WINGS OF AN EAGLE

*An Anthology of Caroline Preachers
with 60 Extracts from their Sermons*

Edited by

G. LACEY MAY

*The Minister hath the wings of an eagle, that every
soul in the congregation may see as much as he sees,
that is a particular interest in all the mercies of God
and the merits of Christ. (Donne, Sermon XLIV)*

LONDON
S·P·C·K
1955

First published in England in 1955 by
S · P · C · K
Northumberland Avenue, London, W.C.2
Printed and Bound in England by
Hazell Watson and Viney Ltd.
Aylesbury and London

To
My Dear Wife

CONTENTS

CONTENTS

CONTENTS

CONTENTS

FOREWORD

The seventeenth century has handed down to our nation a massive religious literature. Most of it, being narrowly controversial, and withal abusive, is now unreadable.

But amongst its many writers a few great names stand head and shoulders above the rest—mostly of Anglo-Catholic preachers. From Bishop Andrewes' time there was a real succession of great Anglican preachers whose sermons still can stir the intellect and move the heart. Donne, Jeremy Taylor, and a few of their successors, are still alive, and likely in any age to find a circle of appreciative readers. From their sermons, too long for modern taste, I offer here quotations which, though short, are long enough to give a reader glimpses of their eloquence and power.

In quoting I have tried to keep carefully to the preacher's exact words. But I have used modern spelling and have adopted modern punctuation, since seventeenth-century writers used a multitude of commas and colons which puzzle and sometimes even mislead the twentieth-century reader. The descriptive titles given to the quotations are generally of my own framing. At the end of the sermon extracts is a list of their various sources.

In the hope that readers of this book may be moved to desire larger draughts of seventeenth-century preachers' wisdom, I print a list of some of the books which deal with them and their times and which may, I hope, be useful to that end.

G. L. M.

3 June 1955

CAROLINE PREACHING

In 1920 Mr L. Pearsall Smith did the public great service by his *Donne's Sermons: Selected Passages*. I should like to feel that I am doing a similar service by this selection of more passages from Donne and from several other great Caroline preachers, whose sermons are hard to come by except in cumbrous and rather ancient editions —Lancelot Andrewes, Mark Frank, John Hales, Isaac Barrow, John Cosin, Henry Hammond, and Jeremy Taylor.

These are Catholic preachers as well as Caroline, for their sermons are based foursquare upon the dogmatic faith of Heaven come to earth to raise earth to Heaven.

The seventeenth century had a multitude of preachers not of this kind, mostly concerned with contemporary and passing controversies. But the men of our choice taught with obvious joy and undiverted purpose the whole Faith. From these I have chosen sixty passages characteristic of their robust outlook.

The choice has not been easy. A reader who travels through many volumes of Caroline sermons emerges from them almost stunned by splendour of thought and speech, by a mixture of resonant thunder and exhilarating fireworks. W. H. Hutton, writing of Henry Hammond, perhaps the mildest of our chosen preachers, says that his sermons make a marked contrast with "the gloomy splendours of Donne and the oriental exuberance of Jeremy Taylor".

Donne is often gloomy, because his powerful imagination led him to see such subjects as death, judgement, and hell (which he pictured as the horror of losing God) as of tremendous and universal import. Yet his gloom rises to splendour, because his intellect, always restless and piercing, has meditated deeply enough upon these great facts of the Christian faith to find them firmly based upon God's unchanging nature of forgiving love. Jeremy Taylor, on the other hand, is exuberant because, though buffeted by constant adversity, his faith learnt too that all learning and all beauty spring from the wisdom and beauty of God.

The seventeenth century, in England as in France, has been called the golden age of preaching. Firstly, it produced many outstanding preachers; secondly, there was an immense desire to hear preaching; and thirdly, it was an era of acute religious controversy, stirring great interest in sermons.

The first part of the century was marked by "witty" preachers on metaphysical subjects. "Witty" did not mean "facetious". It meant that a preacher—to pay the gospel, as he supposed, its due honour—summoned up all his "wit", his knowledge, ingenuity, and learning. So he illustrated his preaching by striking and frequent quotations from Scripture, history, natural history, the ancient classics, the apostolic Fathers, and even heathen philosophers and mythology.

The intention of this method was right enough, the preacher purposing to show that everything in history, legend, or nature revealed somehow the wisdom and power of God. When, however, as with some preachers, it was used to display the speaker's wisdom rather than God's, it followed the example of the Greek sophists and became more worldly than spiritual. When, as often happened, it was carried to excess in minute symbolic interpretation of Holy Writ (learnt from the early Fathers) or in arguments based on foolish legend or the doings of mythological beasts, its purpose became drowned in a tangle of absurdity which neither educated nor edified the hearer.

These eccentricities, or ornate illustrations of argument, became gradually less acceptable as scientific knowledge increased, and as the influence of the Royal Society encouraged by Charles II affected both literature and preaching.

Another feature of "witty" preachers was their love of dissecting their sermon text to discover every jot of interpretation that ingenuity could find. This George Herbert called "crumbling the text"; others called it "jugglery". Though many devout preachers—Andrewes and Donne in particular—were prone to this method, its weaknesses became apparent, and simpler preaching developed. Thus Donne is more lucid than Andrewes, and Jeremy Taylor more lucid than Donne.

Donne's biographer, Izaak Walton, describes him as "a preacher in earnest, weeping sometimes for his auditory, sometimes with them, always preaching to himself, like an angel from the cloud, but in none; carrying some, as St Paul was, to heaven in holy raptures, and enticing others by a sacred art and courtship to amend their lives: here picturing a vice so as to make it ugly to those that practised it; and a virtue to make it beloved, even by those that loved it not; and all this with a most particular grace and an unexpressible addition of comeliness".

Jeremy Taylor, preaching about thirty years after Donne, "learned, original, and often impassioned" and quoting abundantly from every imaginable source, was rather easier to follow than Donne; his language, more fluent, was also simpler. He, like most preachers of the time, thought little of preaching two hours at a stretch.

Sir James Stephen (*Essays in Ecclesiastical Biography*) indicts the seventeenth-century preachers of not caring to instruct artisans and peasants—"Jewell and Bull, Hall and Donne, Hooker and Jeremy Taylor lived and wrote for their peers and for future ages, but not for the commonalty of their own".

This was true (they never mention the poor) though, after all, the educated needed preachers no less than the poor. So Lancelot Andrewes preached to King and Court, Donne to educated listeners at St Paul's, and Jeremy Taylor to Lord Carbery's household in their Welsh mansion. We are left with little knowledge of the sermons preached by the ordinary parish priest to his rural or artisan congregation. If we accept Richard Baxter's description of the lazy, non-preaching clergy of the villages surrounding his boyhood, we may perhaps see one great reason for the English Church collapsing so easily before the Puritan onslaught.

What was really needed to counter that attack was a thousand parish priests throughout England using year by year George Herbert's method of preaching as described by Izaak Walton. The Bemerton saint gave his small rustic congregation, Sunday by Sunday, simple instructions on the Gospel for the Sunday, on the meaning of the festivals, fast-days, and Prayer Book services —instructions well within his hearers' grasp, tender, touching, and paternal.[1] But was not such teaching rare?

On the other hand, the Puritans, more alert than the orthodox clergy, were greatly given to abusive controversial preaching. "The pulpit", says Jeremy Taylor in his preface to the *Golden Grove*, "are fallen under the harrows and saws of impertinent preachers, who think that all religion is a sermon, and all sermons ought to be libels against truth and old governors." Hooker (*Eccl. Pol.* V. 81, 11) had said much the same thing; the pulpit had ousted the altar.[2]

Bitterness of heart conduces neither to personal devotion nor to spiritual preaching. J. B. Mozley, in his masterly essay on Laud, could write of the Puritan lecturers: "Their style of preaching was coarse to a degree which could hardly be credited now, and which absolutely prevents us from making quotations." The greatest Puritan preacher, Richard Baxter, deprecated

[1] See also Herbert's own account in *A Priest to the Temple*, Ch. VII.

[2] Thus Strafford in Ireland in 1638 writes to Laud his surprise that James Ussher, devout and learned Archbishop of Armagh, had a pulpit in his private chapel, but *no altar*.

such preaching, and complained that some Calvinists had no love of God. No doubt the best Puritans agreed with him.

The best Puritans benefited the nation by inculcating higher morals. Some of them combated popular sins or fancied sins; and a kind of sermon grew up which was a vivid description of sins or sinners more in the nature of character-sketches than of Gospel discourses.

The great difference between Catholic and Puritan sermons sprang from their differing conceptions of religion. To the latter the idea of a universal Church mattered far less than individual salvation in the home or parish. Dr W. F. Mitchell in his scholarly book, *English Pulpit Oratory from Andrewes to Tillotson*, says that to the Puritan "The greatest miracle in the Universe was not the incarnation or the passion of the Saviour, but that God should have elected him 'before all worlds' to 'sit with Christ in heavenly places', and, as one of the 'saints', to judge the rest of mankind." So it is not surprising to find Bunyan's hero apparently little concerned with his wife's and children's salvation, so long as he himself could escape damnation.

In other words, the Puritan preachers started from man rather than from God. The Incarnation meant so little to them that they sought to eliminate Christmas Day as a festival, and resented any conception of the Church and her sacraments as "an extension of the incarnation". They had a horror of the word "Catholic": to them both Roman and English Catholicism savoured of hell-fire. "The English Church", says Dr Hensley

Henson in his *Puritanism in England*, "succeeded to the abhorrence which had been felt towards the Church of Rome."

Seventeenth-century Anglo-Catholicism, on the other hand, though it had its own faults, believed in a continuous revelation of God's purposes for mankind from Abraham to their own times. Their preachers dwelt upon the worship, love, and veneration due to God for all that from creation—and especially the Incarnation—he had done for man. The Puritan rejection of divine Church and sacraments seemed to them a wanton ingratitude to the generous love of God's magnanimity to fallen man.

It seems fitting here to note the extraordinary lack of bitterness which marks these Caroline sermons—a feature almost unique in the literature of the age. The century was what we moderns would call an era of persecution. Every preacher in this book lived, and his sermons were preached, against a background of religious persecution. At its beginning Bishop Andrewes, the first of our chosen preachers, was called by King James to undertake an endless controversy against the scheming of Romanists to regain their lost political and religious ascendancy; and only four years before Isaac Barrow, last preacher in our list, died in 1677, the infamous Test Act, expressly purposed to suppress Nonconformity, was passed by a Royalist Parliament; and the repeal of Nonconformist disabilities was not enacted till 1718. Thus the whole century saw England in permanent and bitter religious controversy.

Historians have somewhat inconsistently made Laud the *bête noire* of persecution. But between Roman plotting on the one hand and Puritan hatred and scurrility on the other, he was bound to punish severely those who sought to break the peace of Church or State. John Buchan, always a liberal thinker, points out in his *Oliver Cromwell* that scurrilous pamphleteers like Prynne, Bastwick, and Burton would, a century earlier, have lost their heads, not their ears.

Throughout Europe there was no thought of religious toleration, no government which did not seek to suppress religious hostility by force. Calvin a century before had burnt Servetus as a Unitarian. The Pilgrim Fathers, when once in America, scourged Quakers. Cromwell, who professed toleration, ordered his soldiers to kill every Popish priest they met, and rejoiced at wholesale massacres of Catholics at Drogheda and Wexford. Under his rule an Anglican priest preached or taught or used the Church Prayer Book, even privately, on pain of banishment. There existed a rabid hate of the slightest hint of Catholicism. Lord Brooke, a Puritan leader in the House of Lords, sailing once down the Thames, shook his fist at St Paul's and swore that he would not rest till he saw it dismantled stone by stone. Not long after, he lost his life in leading an armed attack against Lichfield Cathedral. John Evelyn's *Diary* gives a vivid account of how, when he and friends were making their communion on Christmas Day, a troop of musketeers burst in, and levelled muskets at the heads of the kneeling worshippers. These were taken prisoner, and Evelyn, taken before a magistrate, was rated for observing "the superstitious time of the Nativity".

It is against this background of hatred, the desecration of cathedrals, the ousting of many devout and learned parish priests, as "malignants" or "unlearned", from their benefices, that a reader must appraise our orthodox Caroline sermons.

Though the question of disputed religious authority dominated the century, and might well have dominated all preachers, the great Caroline preachers, however they had suffered, are singularly free from personal bitterness. The occasional attacks on Papist doctrines in Donne's sermons were without malice, and were natural enough when Spanish and French ambassadors had great influence at the English Court. Jeremy Taylor, it is true, sorrowing in his Welsh exile, could write: "I have lived to see religion painted upon banners, and thrust out of churches . . . and God to be worshipped, not as he is, the Father of our Lord Jesus Christ, an afflicted Prince, the King of suffering . . . but rather as the Lord of hosts." But such words were instinct, not with personal hatred, but with the anguish of mind natural in a devout Churchman who had an intense love for his suffering Church. We see the same distress of mind, linked with a courageous humility, in Laud's noble sermon from the scaffold. Not their own tribulations, but the shattering of Church worship and teaching, distressed these sufferers most.

The truth is that the time for toleration was not yet. Successive pleas by Milton, Jeremy Taylor, and Richard

Baxter were brushed aside by the exigencies of current politics or religious rivalry.

When the Restoration came, we must confess that some of the Restoration bishops concurred with the persecuting policy of a revengeful Royalist Parliament. Yet not only did our great preachers refrain from language of hatred or bitterness, but some of them, such as Hales, Chillingworth, and Isaac Barrow, preached and wrote on the side of toleration. Strangely enough, their influence was not effective until the time of William III, a man indifferent alike to morality or religion.

It is fair to add that before toleration came, Puritanism shone with noble lustre in the saintliness of Richard Baxter, and the sweet charity of Bunyan, before their persecutors; whilst many Nonconformist ministers courageously and faithfully served their London congregations during the Plague.

I have written here nothing of great Puritan preachers: indeed, little can be said. The intense concern of the early Puritans against episcopacy and the ordinary ceremonial of the Church could produce vehement controversialists, but not good preachers. An envenomed heart does not conduce to spirituality in the pulpit.[1]

Secondly, though it is greatly to the credit of Puritan preachers that they insisted upon such plain sermons as could be understood by the common people, they carried this so far as to make their sermons extremely dull. Deliberately avoiding all learned, classical, or secular

[1] Cf. *infra*, Extract 54.

illustrations or quotations,[1] and any attempt at style, they have left behind them no sermons to interest a reader.

"The prevailing tone of such sermons", says W. F. Mitchell, "is one of gloomy dogma and censoriousness, and even so gifted and lively a writer as Bunyan, if we may judge from the solitary specimen which we possess of his sermons . . . was heavy and dull." Mitchell names ten of their prominent preachers—"mighty men who invited armies to battle in the name of the Lord or denounced curses against the hesitant or the temperate— not one of these excites the faintest interest in us at the present day". Even the sermons of Richard Baxter make dull reading.

The sermons of Catholic and Puritan preachers alike are soaked in Biblical thought and language. They found this easy, for not they only, but also their hearers knew their Bibles. When Jeremy Taylor preaches of the power of prayer to save in every emergency, he does not trouble to tell Bible stories, but refers to them without quoting names. In our Extract 50, for instance, he says that the prayers of holy men appease God's wrath, and at once we remember Abraham's intercession for Lot; that prayer cures sicknesses, and we remember Hezekiah; that prayer procures the help of angels, and we think of the boy Ishmael's prayer; that it procures pardon, and we think of the Penitent Thief; that it stays the sun, and

---

[1] The tradition died hard. Only forty-five years ago, one of my friends, after preaching in Lincoln Minster, was rebuked by an aged archdeacon: "I was surprised to hear you quote Shakespeare in your sermon; *never quote a heathen writer in the pulpit.*" G. L. M.

our mind reverts to Joshua's prayer; that it checks or produces rain, and Elijah's prayers come to mind; that it unlocks the womb and quenches the power of fire, and at once we remember Hannah, and the Three in the Fiery Furnace; that it stops the mouths of lions, and Daniel is remembered; that it reconciles weak faculties to violent persecutions, and (as Shakespeare expected his audiences to remember the Apocryphal story of Susannah in his "second Daniel") we realize that Taylor meant his congregation to recall the mother and her seven dauntless sons before the persecutor Antiochus.

Throughout this whole passage on prayer the preacher mentions no name. To how many modern congregations would such a series of theological statements suggest the corresponding Biblical stories? The interest, and the power, of all seventeenth-century preachers were enhanced by the fact that, as J. R. Green declares, the Reformation, whatever its mistakes, had made England a Bible-loving nation.

The Church's faithful repetition of Scripture and Psalms in all her post-Reformation services—in spite of the futility of many lections chosen—has immensely strengthened English religion. Laud's seven surviving sermons, says W. H. Hutton,[1] seem inclined to historical rather than theological interest; but they have a second feature. He "continually refers to the psalms and lessons of the day; he was so familiar with the Church's daily services that he naturally took them as providing each

---

[1] *Cambridge History of English Literature*, Vol. VII, p. 159.

day with its lesson from God, and that lesson should be the first he would employ for application or illustration. This was personal to the man; it occurs again and again in his diary and tinges his prayers." So was it too with Charles I.

Great Caroline preachers, being of the Laudian school, found it natural to strengthen their sermons with per-petual Scripture (the Puritans, too, were right here, had they but handled their material better). But this was as followers, not of Andrewes and Laud, but of Catholic custom from the Church's beginning.

They were able to do this the more effectively because they possessed the power of *a trained and consecrated imagination*, applied vividly to the Biblical writings for the strengthening of their own and their hearers' personal relationship with God.

In this use of visual imagination the Caroline preacher was always strong. Modern preachers, for lack of it, and religious writers, are fond of using abstract terms, thus helping to empty church pews, since the ordinary Englishman can make little of abstract conceptions. A preacher may earnestly exhort his hearers to lead a "spiritual life", but his people, for lack of definite instruc-tion, do not know what he means. If he would urge them to "live daily as near to God as possible", and tell them how to do so, they would more easily find a basic con-ception for daily Christian living.

A Caroline preacher seldom made the mistake of speaking abstractly. His imagination, fed on Biblical imagery, attached, as our Lord did in parable and exhortation, the details of natural visible life to the spiritual realities. Luminous, vivid, even gay language can inflame a hearer's imagination as a spark sets fire to dry kindling; cloudy speech effects just as much as, and no more than, a passing cloud.

Let us recall a few instances of the Caroline preacher's use of his imagination. Jeremy Taylor, speaking of the need of a quiet mind for effective prayer, pictures a lark rising at dawn, to sing aloft, but beaten down by the force of a boisterous wind till, panting, she is forced to come to earth again and rest until the wind has ceased. Just so, Taylor tells us, must a man quieten all anger or selfish passion in his heart if his prayers are to rise to God.

Or take Mark Frank's sermon in which he pictures the coming of Christ into Jerusalem, accompanied by a rejoicing crowd with Hosannas strewing palm-leaves before his ass's feet. Some go before, says Frank, and they are holy prophets, priests, and kings of the Old Testament; those who are gathered round our Lord are the holy Apostles; whilst those who follow are members of the Church of every age—martyrs, saints, missionaries, and humble men and women of faith and prayer. Each of his listeners, he tells them, can, and must, join in that numberless crowd, loving, praising, and following their adored Master. In such concrete, yet imaginative, speech a preacher moves his hearers' hearts. And Frank's pictures are the more effective because drawn—especially those connected with the Incarnation—not as isolated scenes, but as each taking its due place and proportion in the symmetry of the whole Faith.

Or take at random a short intimate picture by Donne. Where many a modern preacher vaguely talks about "difficulties in prayer", Donne *pictures* them, takes his hearers into his study where, as he kneels before God with the best of intentions, his prayers are broken by thoughts of yesterday's pleasures, to-morrow's dangers, and "a straw under my knee, a noise in mine ear, a light in mine eye, an any thing, a nothing, a fancy . . . in my brain" may trouble him in his prayers. Every listener here at once recognizes himself, his own difficulties in time of praying.

It is by such concrete use of the imagination that the Gospel stories seek to help us towards God. We can picture, as we kneel in meditation, how St Peter, after his miraculous draught, knelt that early dawn before his Master's feet, startled and awed into penitence by a Lord mighty to forgive and to save. Donne, if he had preached on that subject, would have left not Peter, but his hearers, kneeling in adoration.

Bishop Cosin, in simple concrete language describing his aged sister's calm and prayerful preparation for approaching death, sets our minds and hearts to wondering and praying about our own meeting with death.

The point of all these illustrations is that the use of the imagination in grasping divine truth brings a rich reward.

Mark Frank, whom we have already noticed, is a master in using his imagination over the sacred material of Biblical scenes. First he allows the Holy Spirit to limn to his own mind a vivid picture of the surroundings and persons, that with him his hearers may see the whole picture after him. To use Donne's vivid phrase, he "hath the wings of an eagle, that every soul in the congregation may see as much as he sees". Seeing in the story (or passage) and its implications the underlying purpose of God, he introduces both scene and divine purpose to the waiting and receptive minds of his hearers. As Pieter Brueghel's canvases glow with colour and action, so does Frank's Biblical pageant, but sanctified to the divine purpose. Through crowds and processions of apostles, angels, saints, and rejoicing children, he leaves his hearers—and, to-day, his readers—isolated with God. And his fervid luminous scenes—not least those connected with the Incarnation—are not isolated episodes, but fall into their due place and proportion in the ordered sequence of the Church's story.

Thus, says Henry Hammond in one of his sermons, can teachers of Bible truths "press into God's cabinet secrets, invade the book of life, and oversee and divulge to all men *abscondita Domini nostri*". When a preacher of any time and place has learnt this lesson, he no longer preaches to his congregation vague and abstract conceptions. Before he leaves his pulpit, they will have caught at least some vision of God.

But what if the preacher or teacher seldom, or never, makes time to soar in secret imagination, to take home to himself the secrets of God? Can the blind lead the blind? Is not the jejuneness and dullness of much modern preaching due to the fact that the preacher has not knelt humbly and prayerfully before God in the preparing of his message? The eagle (Deut. 32. 11) which "stirreth up her nest, fluttereth over her young, spreadeth abroad her wings, taketh them, beareth them on her wings", can do so only if she has already learnt to soar into the empyrean. The preacher's heart and mind must mount high enough for himself to be touched with the divine flame.

This power to portray to the mind scenes which move the heart and stir the will to a deeper penitence and love of God is confessedly in part a poetic gift in its harmonizing the concrete with the ineffable. Milton in his "Nativity Ode" first pictures the heathen deities fleeing, and all nature moved, at the birth of the infant Christ. But this wholly abstract picture must needs end, and blend, with a more concrete presentation:

> "*See! the Virgin blest*
> *Hath laid her Babe to rest.*
> Time is our tedious song should here have ending:
> Heaven's youngest-teeméd star
> Hath fixed her polished car,
> Her sleeping Lord with handmaid lamp attending;
> *And all about the courtly stable*
> *Bright-harnessed Angels sit in order serviceable!*"

After all, such use of his imagination every devout layman must make as he reads a Bible passage, and listens for God's message over his daily meditation. The

preacher needs to do the same in preparing for his sermons. If he does not thus use, and enrich, his imagination,
how can he touch, or enrich, the imagination of his
hearers? However diffident he may feel as to his imaginative powers, he must realize that an undeveloped spiritual
imagination can be inspired and strengthened by daily
devotional musing over Bible passages or scenes in the
presence of God with faithful prayer and a surrendered
heart. The best Caroline sermons show signs of being
the result of faithfulness to this practice of reading the
mind of God.

To this end meditation must be sincere. Meditation,
with its method of visualizing Bible scenes or events, is
often given little chance of helping the soul, because it
is looked upon as a more or less formal act of obedience
to conscience. A man, once taught to meditate, feels that
he must do so, even if it means a meditation scrambling,
hasty, and careless.

Hurried meditation has little value. If with less leisure
for it than the Carolines had, we must see that our meditations are *deliberate*, or they will fail to link the human
with the infinite. Even a meditation of but fifteen minutes
must be begun by the purposive laying aside of haste. If
entered upon in this resolute spirit of quietude, and in an
attitude of humble receptiveness to God's voice, it can,
and will, enrich the whole personality and power of the
preacher.

In the *Sunday Times*, 21 November 1954, Dr Albert
Schweitzer, discussing the power of the human spirit to
achieve lasting world peace, wrote: "The full strength of

the human spirit was revealed to us in the seventeenth and eighteenth centuries. It was through its agency that Europe was dragged forth from the Middle Ages, and superstition, witchcraft-trials, and the torture-chamber were abolished. The spirit of man created new marvels in their place."

Are not the great missionary's words true? And has not this advance of the human spirit been largely achieved by the genius, charity, and faith of the Caroline preachers?

LANCELOT ANDREWES (1555–1626)

Lancelot Andrewes first rose to eminence when at Cambridge, as Master of Pembroke Hall, he opposed Thomas Cartwright, whose Puritan theology was then predominant there. Andrewes was chaplain-in-ordinary to Queen Elizabeth, but received no preferment from her, because he protested against her unscrupulous alienation of Church revenues.

James I, however, delighted in his preaching, and made him successively Bishop of Chichester, Ely, and Winchester. His erudite spiritual sermons were in great favour at Court; and his discourses and saintly character served as some deterrent to the coarseness of James and his courtiers.

Andrewes is admitted into this collection of Caroline preachers, as being "the last of the 'witty' preachers", whose chief characteristic was a display of great learning expressed in quaint conceits, many quotations, and a closely detailed exposition of Scripture texts. Andrewes was a link between them and the more lucid preachers like Donne and Jeremy Taylor.

His style, often artificial and crabbed, makes his sermons no easy reading to-day. A courtier, being asked by James what he thought of an Andrewes sermon, replied: "He did play with his text, as a Jack-an-apes does, who takes up a thing and tosses it, and plays with it, and then he takes up another and plays a little with it. Here's a pretty thing, and there's a pretty thing."

But the deep seriousness of his preaching profoundly influenced his greater successor, John Donne.

1. THE WORD MADE FLESH

"The Word was made flesh" . . . What flesh? The flesh of an infant. What, *Verbum infans*, the Word an infant? The Word, and not able to speak a word? How evil agreeth this! This he put up. How born, how entertained? In a stately palace, cradle of ivory, robes of estate? No; but a stable for his palace, a manger for his cradle, poor clouts for his array. This was his beginning. Follow him farther, if any better afterward; what flesh afterward? *Sudans et algens*, in cold and heat, hungry and thirsty, faint and weary. Is his end any better? that maketh up all; what flesh then? *Cujus livore sanati*, black and blue, bloody and swollen, rent and torn, the thorns and nails sticking in his flesh; and such flesh he was made. A great *factum* certainly, and much to be made of. To have been made *caput Angelorum* had been an abasement; to be *minoratus Angelis* is more; but, to be *novissimus vivorum*, "in worst case of all men", nay, "a worm and no man"; so to be born, so arrayed, and so housed, and so handled—there is not the meanest flesh but is better. So to be made, and so unmade; to take it on, and lay it off, with so great indignity: weigh it and wonder at it that ever he would endure to be made flesh, and to be made it on this manner. What was it made the Word thus to be made flesh? *Non est lex hominis ista*, "flesh would never have been brought to it". It was God, and in God nothing but love. . . .

Good hope we now have that he being now flesh, all

3

flesh may come to him to present him with their requests. Time was when they fled from him, but *ad factum carnem jam veniet omnis caro*. For since he dwelt amongst us, all may resort to him—yea, even sinners; and of them it is said, *Hic recipit peccatores, et comedit cum eis*; "he receiveth them, receiveth them even to his table".

A second hope, that seeing he hath made our flesh his tabernacle, he will not suffer this of ours—the same with that of his—to fall down quite and come to nothing; the same he dwelleth in himself not to perish utterly; but repair it again and raise it out of the dust. So that *insuper caro nostra requiescet in spe*, "our very body may rest in hope", to be restored again, and "made like to his glorious Body".

2. CHRISTMAS JOY

Luke 2. 10: "The angel said unto them, Be not afraid; for behold, I bring you good tidings of great joy, which shall be to all people."

This is *evangelizo gaudium*, "this is joy indeed".

But even in joy there be divers degrees. All are not of one size. Some there are lesser; some, as this here, *gaudium magnum*. The fire is as the fuel is, and the joy is as the matter is. There is not like joy to a shepherd when his ewe brings him a lamb, as when his wife brings him a son; yet that of a lamb is a joy, such as it is. But then, if that son should prove to be *princeps pastorum*, "the chief shepherd in all the land", that were somewhat more. But then, if he should prove to be a Cyrus, or a David, a prince, then certainly it were another manner of joy, *gaudium magnum* indeed. As the matter is, so is the joy. If great the benefit, great the person, then great the joy. And here the benefit is great, none greater; as much as the saving of us all, as much as all our lives and souls are worth; therefore great. And the person great, none so great—it is the Lord himself—therefore *primae magnitudinis*, great even as he is. . . . Therefore well said the angel, *Evangelizo gaudium magnum*.

And great it may be *intensive*, in the parties themselves; yet not great *extensive*, nor extend itself to many, not be *gaudium magnum populo*. . . . In other joys it falls out as Esay tells, "multiply the nation, and ye shall not increase

5

their joy"; for that which one wins another loses: but this joy, the joy of *Puer natus est nobis*, in it "they shall all rejoice before thee, as men make merry in harvest, and be joyful as men that divide the spoil". "In harvest"; and a good harvest all the country is the better for. "At a spoil"; wherein every one hath his share. That is *gaudium populi*, and such is this. Well figured in the place of his birth, an inn, which is *domus populi*, "open to all passengers" that will take it up; *juris publici*, "wherein every one hath right". Yea, and the most common part the inn. For though they sort themselves and have every one their several chambers, in the stable all have interest; that is common. And as the place public, so is the benefit, and so is the joy public of his birth: Christmas joy right; all fare the better for this day. *Salus populi* is the best, and so is *gaudium populi* too; and every good mind will like it so much the better that all the people have their part in it. . . .

Men may talk what they will, but sure there is no joy in the world to the joy of a man saved; no joy so great, no news so welcome, as to one ready to perish, in case of a lost man, to hear of one that will save him. In danger of perishing by sickness, to hear of one will make him well again; by sentence of the law, of one with a pardon to save his life; by enemies, of one that will rescue and set him in safety. Tell any of these, assure them but of a Saviour, it is the best news he ever heard in his life.

There is joy in the name of a Saviour. And even this way, this Child is a Saviour too. *Potest hoc facere, sed hoc non est opus ejus*, "This he can do, but this is not his work"; a farther matter there is, a greater salvation he came for. And it may be we need not any of these; we are not presently sick, in no fear of the law, in no danger of enemies. And it may be, if we were, we fancy to ourselves to be relieved some other way. But that which he came for, that saving we need all; and none but he can help us to it. We have therefore all cause to be glad for the Birth of this Saviour.

John 20. 11–17

(a) St Mark is express for it, that Christ was no sooner risen this day but "he appeared first of all to Mary Magdalene"; which first appearing of his is here by St John extended, and set down at large.

The sum of it is, 1. The seeking Christ dead; 2. The finding him alive.

The manner of it is, that Mary Magdalene staying still by the sepulchre, first she saw a vision of angels, and after, she saw Christ himself. Saw him, and was herself made an angel by him, a good angel to carry the evangel, the first good and joyful tidings of his rising again from the dead. And this was a great honour, all considered, to serve in an angel's place. To do that at his resurrection, his second birth, that at his first birth an angel did. An angel first published that, Mary Magdalene brought first notice of this. As he to the shepherds, so she to the apostles, the pastors of Christ's flock, by them to be spread abroad to the ends of the world.

To look a little into it. 1. Mary is the name of a woman; 2. Mary Magdalene of a sinful woman.

That to a woman first—it agreeth well to make even with Eve; that as by a woman came the first news of death, so by a woman also might come the first notice of the resurrection from the dead. And the place fits well, for in a garden they came both.

That to a sinful woman first—that also agrees well.

To her first that most needed it; most needed it, and so first sought it. And it agrees well, he be first found of her that first sought him; even in that respect she was to be respected.

In which two there is opened unto us "a gate of hope", two great leaves, as it were; one, that no infirmity of sex —for a woman we see; the other, that no enormity of sin—for a sinful woman, one that had the blemish that she went under the common name of *peccatrix*, as notorious and famous in that kind; that neither of these shall debar any to have their part in Christ and in his resurrection; any, that shall seek him in such sort as she did. For either of these *non obstante*, nay notwithstanding both these, she had the happiness to see his angels—and that was no small favour; to see Christ himself, and that first of all, before all others to see and salute him; and to receive a commission from him of *vade et dic*, to "go and tell", that is as it were to be an Apostle, and that to the Apostles themselves, to bring them the first good news of Christ's rising again.

(*b*) I cannot here pass over two more characters of her love, that so you may have the full ten I promised.

One, in *si tu sustulisti eum*, in her *eum*, in her "him". Him? Which him? Her affections seem so to transport her, as she says no man knows what. To one, a mere stranger to her, and she to him, she talks of one thrice under the term of "him"; "if thou hast taken him away, tell me where thou hast laid him, and I will fetch him"; him, him, and him, and never names him or tells us who he is.

This is *soloecismus amoris*, an irregular speech, but love's own dialect. "Him" is enough with love: who knows not who that is? It supposes every body, all the world bound to take notice of him whom we look for, only by saying "him", though we never tell his name, nor say a word more. *Amor, quem ipse cogitat, neminem putans ignorare.*

The other is in her *ego tollam*: if he would tell her where he had laid him, she would go fetch him, that she would. Alas, poor woman, she was not able to lift him. There are more than one, or two either, allowed to the carrying of a corpse.

As for his, it had more than a hundred pound weight of myrrh and other odours upon it, beside the poise of a dead body. She could not do it. Well, yet she would do it though. *O mulier, non mulier*, saith Origen, for *ego tollam* seems rather the speech of a porter, or of some lusty strong fellow at least, than of a silly weak woman. But love makes women more than women, at least it makes them have νοῦν ὑπὲρ ἰσχύν, the courage above the strength, far. Never measures her own forces, no burden too heavy, no assay too hard for love, *et nihil erubescit nisi nomen difficultatis*, "and is not ashamed of any thing but that any thing should be too hard or too heavy for it".

4. THE CHURCH PENITENT

It is good you know it, the fast [Lent] so delivered, and by the Church ever and every where so kept. . . . And sure in general, that this power should remain in the Church to prescribe us set times was most behoveful. Every man, so we would have it, to be left to himself for prayer, fasting, Sacrament, nay for religion too now and all? For God's sake, let it not be so, let us not be left altogether to ourselves, no, not in prayer! Private prayer doth well; but let us be ordered to come to Church, and do it there, Pharisees, Publicans, Peter and John, and all; let us have our days appointed and our hours set for it. If all were left to us, God knows I durst not promise what should become of prayer itself. The like I say for the Sacrament; let us have a *cum* when to come to that too: and so for fasting; fast privately in God's name, but, hear you, let not the Church trust to that. Nor she hath not held it wisdom so to do; but as in both them, prayer and the Sacrament, so in this holds us to our order of days and times established. Then if we keep, so it is: otherwise, were it not for the Church's times, I doubt there would be taken scarce any time at all. . . . The rest are matters of discipline rather than doctrine: 1. the number of forty; 2. the season of the year; 3. the manner of abstinence. . . .

That which hath been said is for some set time at large, for a *cum*; but why this *cum* at this time now? Why forty days? Why before Easter? Why this fast? It is of all hands confessed, that ordained it was as a part of the discipline of repentance; and much was done in it about public penitents. Yet not for them only; but even with them out of the bowels of a mother the Church herself would become a penitent, and have all her children do the like. Herself become one; for the whole body of the Church hath her faults beside the private offences of every particular member, for which there was a several set sacrifice in the Law. For us to become penitents likewise; for who knows whether we be not as faulty in private as they, the open penitents in public? As great sinners as they, though not known for such?

5. LOOKING UPON THE CRUCIFIED

Zech. 12. 10. "They shall look upon me, whom they have pierced."

It was sin that gave him these wounds, so it was love to us that made him receive them, being otherwise able enough to have avoided them all. So that he was pierced with love no less than with grief, and it was that wound of love made him so constantly to endure all the other. Which love we may read in the palms of his hands, as the Fathers express it out of Esay 49. 16; for "in the palms of his hands he hath graven us", that he might not forget us. And the print of the nails in them, are as capital letters to record his love towards us. For Christ pierced on the cross is *liber charitatis*, "the very book of love" laid open before us. And again, this love of his we may read in the cleft of his heart. *Quia clavus penetrans factus est nobis clavis reserans*, saith Bernard, *ut pateant nobis viscera per vulnera*: "the point of the spear serves us instead of a key, letting us through his wounds see his very bowels", the bowels of tender love and most kind compassion, that would for us endure to be so entreated. That if the Jews that stood by said truly of him at Lazarus' grave, *Ecce quomodo dilexit cum!* when he shed a few tears out of his eyes; much more truly may we say of him, *Ecce quomodo dilexit nos!* seeing him shed both water and blood, and that in great plenty, and that out of his heart.

Which sight ought to pierce us with love too, no less than before it did with sorrow. With one, or with both, for both have power to pierce; but especially love, which except it had entered first and pierced him, no nail or spear could ever have entered. Then let this be the third,[1] *respice et dilige*; "look and be pierced with love of him" that so loved thee, that he gave himself in this sort to be pierced for thee.

And forasmuch as it is Christ his own self that, resembling his passion on the cross to the brazen serpent lift up in the wilderness, maketh a correspondence between their beholding and our believing—for so it is John 3. 14—we cannot avoid, but must needs make that an effect too; even *respice et crede*. And well may we believe and trust him, whom looking a little before we have seen so constantly loving us. For the sight of that love maketh credible unto us whatsoever in the whole Scripture is affirmed unto us of Christ, or promised in his Name; so that believe it, and believe all. Neither is there any time wherein with such cheerfulness or fullness of faith we cry unto him, "My Lord, and my God", as when our eye is fixed upon "the print of the nails, and on the hole in the side" of him that was pierced for us. So that this fourth duty Christ himself layeth upon us, and willeth us from his own mouth, *respice et crede*.

[1] Earlier in his sermon Andrewes has spoken of divers mottoes applicable for beholding Christ's Passion—*respice et transfigere*, "look and be pierced"; *respice et transfige*, "look and pierce your sin". Here he gives a third, *respice et dilige*, "look and love". Later he gives a fourth, *respice et crede*, "look and believe"; and a fifth, *respice et spera*, "look and hope".

And believing this of him, what is there the eye of our hope shall not look for from him? What would not he do for us, that for us would suffer all this? It is St Paul's argument, "If God gave his Son for us, how shall he deny us any thing with him?" That is, *respice et spera*. "Look upon him, and his heart opened, and from that gate of hope promise thyself and look for all manner of things that good are."

Which our expectation is reduced to these two: 1. The deliverance from evil of our present misery; 2. and the restoring to the good of our primitive felicity. By the death of this undefiled Lamb, as by the yearly Passover, look for and hope for a passage out of Egypt, which spiritually is our redemption from the servitude of the power of darkness. And as by the death of the Sacrifice we look to be freed from whatsoever evil, so by the death of the High Priest look we for and hope for restitution to all that is good; even to our forfeited estate in the Land of Promise which is Heaven itself, where is all joy and happiness for evermore. *Respice et spera*, "look and look for"; by the Lamb that is pierced to be freed from all misery, by the High Priest that is pierced fruition of all felicity.

Ps. 78. 34: "When he slew them, then they sought him;
and they returned, and enquired early after God."
(*Cum occideret eos, querebant eum; et revertebantur, et
diluculo veniebant ad eum.*)

"They" shall seek; and the time is set down when they
shall seek, and when you shall not fail but see them seek
that never sought before. *In diebus juventutis*, not then.
Sanus factus est, nor then neither; but *cum occideret*, then
certainly. *Cum occideret*, mark this *cum* when it cometh,
and you shall see them that stood out all their life long
then come in.

(1) The heathen man saw it with his eyes. O, saith
the Persian messenger in Aeschylus, when the Grecian
forces hotly pursued our host, and we must needs venture
over the great water Strymon, frozen then but beginning
to thaw, when an hundred to one we had all died for it
—that is, *cum occideret*, with mine eyes I saw (saith he)
when θεοὺς δέ τις, etc. (Aeschylus, *Persae* 497, *et seq.*).
Of those gallants whom I had heard before so boldly
maintain there was no God to seek; τότ' ηὔχετο λιτᾶισι,
then every one of them on their knees, and full devoutly
praying the ice might hold till they got over. (2) Moses
saw it with his eyes. Pharaoh, who was at high terms,
"Who is the Lord you talk of?" and answered himself,
"he knew none such", nor nothing would do for him:
when *cum occideret* came, he took notice there was a

Lord higher than he; "that that Lord was righteous, and he a wretched sinner" that sought for grace at his hands.

(3) Mark but the shutting up of *dixit insipiens*, their own Psalm, When, saith David, they have in heart sought to persuade themselves, *non est*—seek none, "none there is"; and thereupon "corrupted themselves", and became most loathsome in their lives, "eat up their tenants as they would so many morsels of bread"; made a mock of such holy men as set themselves seriously to seek God; when all is done and *occideret* come, *trepidabant timore ubi non erat timor*, "they shall begin to be afraid, where they held before no fear needed"; and here shall be the last verse of their Psalm; *quis dabit e Sion salutem*, "to wish for the salvation of Sion", which they have so oft derided. "They shall seek", and "then they shall seek".

Till then possibly you shall lose your labour, if you tell them of seeking of God, but and how good it is. They are, saith Jeremy, "like the dromedary of the wilderness", a beast of exceeding swiftness, the female specially: "over hill and dale she goeth", saith the Prophet, "and snuffeth up the air at her pleasure, and who can overtake her? They that seeketh her will not weary themselves till her month." And in her month when she is bagged, then they will find her, and deal with her well enough.

The case is like. Age, sickness, death, are far off; youth, health, and strength possess them; there is no coming to them then. The month, *cum occideret*, is not yet come; but come that once as once it will to all, you shall find *quaerant* will have his place—*fiat*.

It is therefore God's own resolution, thus he resolveth: "I will go", saith he, "and return to my place, till they acknowledge their faults and seek me." And when will that be? He addeth, *in novissimo quaerant me diligenter*, an end will come, and when that cometh "they will seek me diligently", even the best of them.

And even so we are fain to resolve; for our lot is God's lot, and when he sought to them, we go to our place, and there stand till their month, *expectantes aquae motum*, waiting till the destroying angel come and stir the water, and then *quaerent eum* will be worth the seeking after.

Then, according to St Paul's disjunctive, we that all other times *mente excedimus Deo*, at that time *sobrii sumus vobis*. Divinity, which in our ruff is sophism and school-points, and at the best a kind of ecstasy about God, is and shall be then, "the words of truth and soberness". For God and his seeking will have their time; before, if it may be, but if not before, then at the farthest. First or last, all shall confess by seeking God is to be sought. Some before he kill, and happy are they; but "when he killeth", all: hypocrites, heathens, atheists, and all.

JOHN DONNE (1573–1631)

John Donne studied at Oxford and Cambridge in turn, and then at Lincoln's Inn with a view to the Law. Born a Roman Catholic, after long thought and study he joined the Church of England. After a tour on the Continent, he was engaged as a private secretary; but fell into trouble by secretly marrying his patron's niece, Ann More.

Always interested in the controversy between the Church and Romanism, he produced in 1610 a book, *The Proto-Martyr*, of which King James approved so much that he urged Donne to take Holy orders.

After a delay of three years, owing to his feeling of unworthiness, Donne consented, and after Ordination was sent by the King on a political mission to Bohemia.

In 1621 he was appointed Dean of St Paul's, where he won immense popularity and respect as an eloquent and powerful preacher. He died ten years later.

7. PRIDE THE PRIMAL SIN AGAINST GOD

It is not much controverted in the schools, but that the first sin of the angels was pride. But because . . . the danger of man is more in sinking down, than in climbing up, in dejecting, than in raising himself, we must therefor remember, that it is not pride, to desire to be better. *Angeli quaesivereunt id, ad quod pervenissent si stetissent* (Augustine). The angels' sin was pride; but their pride consisted not in aspiring to the best degrees that their nature was capable of: but in this, that they would come to that state by other means than were ordained for it. It could not possibly fall within so pure and clear understandings as the angels were, to think that they could be God; that God could be multiplied; that they who knew themselves to be but new made, could think, not only that they were not made, but that they made all things else; to think that they were God, is impossible, this could not fall into them, though they would be *similes Altissimo*, like the Most High. But this was their pride, and in this they would be like the Most High, that whereas God subsisted in his essence of himself, for those degrees of perfection, which appertained to them, they would have them of themselves; they would stand in their perfection, without any turning towards God, without any further assistance from him; by themselves, and not by means ordained for them. This is the pride that is forbidden man; not that he think well of himself, *In genere suo*, that he value aright the dignity of his nature, in the creation thereof according to the image of God, and the infinite improvement that that nature received, in being assumed by the Son of God; this is not pride, but not to acknowledge that all this dignity in nature, and all that it conduces to, that is, grace here, and glory hereafter, is not only infused by God at first, but sustained by God still, and that nothing in the beginning, or way, or end, is of ourselves, this is pride.

8. HELP OTHERS WITH YOUR INTERCESSIONS

When St Augustine's mother lamented the ill courses that her son took in his youth, still that priest, to whom she imparted her sorrows, said, *Filius istarum lacrymarum, non potest perire*; that son, for whom so good a mother hath shed so many tears, cannot perish: he put it not upon that issue, *filius Dei*, the elect child of God, the son of predestination cannot perish, for at that time, that name was either no name, or would scarce have seemed to have belonged to St Augustine, but the child of these tears, of this devotion cannot be lost. Christ said to the centurion, *Fiat sicut credidisti, Go thy way, and as thou believest, so be it done unto thee, and his servant was healed in the self-same hour*: the master believed, and the servant was healed. Little knowest thou, what thou hast received at God's hands by the prayers of the saints in Heaven, that enwrap thee in their general prayers for the militant Church. Little knowest thou, what the public prayers of the congregation, what the private prayers of particular devout friends, that lament thy carelessness, and negligence in praying for thyself, have wrung and extorted out of God's hands, in their charitable importunity for thee. And therefore, at last, make thyself fit to do for others, that which others, when thou wast unfit to do thyself that office, have done for thee in assisting thee with their prayers. *If thou meet thine enemy's ox, or ass going astray* (says the law) *thou shalt surely bring it back to him again: if thou see the ass of him that hateth thee, lying under his burden, and wouldst forbear to help him, thou shalt surely help him. Estne Deo cura de bobus?* is the Apostle's question, *Hath God care of oxen?* of other men's oxen? How much more of his own sheep? And therefore if thou see one of his sheep, one of thy fellow-Christians, strayed into sins of infirmity, and negligent of himself, join him with thine own soul, in thy prayers to God. Relieve him (if that be that which he needs) with thy prayers for him, and relieve him (if his wants be of another kind) according to his prayers to thee. *Cur apud te homo collega non valeat*, says St Ambrose, Why should not he that is thy colleague, thy fellow-man, as good a man, that is as much a man as thou, made of the same blood, and redeemed with the same blood as thou art, why should not he prevail with thee, so far as to the obtaining of an alms? *Cum apud Deum, servus, et interveniendi meritum, et jus habeat impetrandi*, When some fellow-servant of thine, hath had that interest in God, as by his intercession, and prayers to advance thy salvation, wilt not thou save the life of another man that prays to thee, when perchance thy soul hath been saved by another man, that prayed for thee?

9. THE CATHOLICITY OF THE PSALMS

Ps. 63. 7: "Because thou hast been my help, therefore in the shadow of thy wings will I rejoice."

The Psalms are the manna of the Church. As manna tasted to every man like that he liked best, so do the Psalms minister instruction, and satisfaction, to every man, in every emergency and occasion. David was not only a clear prophet of Christ himself, but a prophet of every particular Christian; he foretells what I, what any shall do, and suffer, and say. And as the whole Book of Psalms is *oleum effusum* (as the spouse speaks of the name of Christ (Cant. 1. 3)), an ointment poured out upon all sorts of sores, a cerecloth that supples all bruises, a balm that searches all wounds; so are there some certain Psalms that are imperial Psalms, that command over all affections, and spread themselves over all occasions, catholic, universal Psalms, that apply themselves to all necessities.

This is one of those; for, of those constitutions which are called apostolical, one is, that the Church should meet every day, to sing this Psalm. And accordingly, St Chrysostom testifies, that it was decreed, and ordained by the primitive Fathers, that no day should pass without the public singing of this Psalm. Under both these obligations (those ancient constitutions, called the Apostle's, and those ancient decrees made by the primitive Fathers) belongs to me, who have my part in the service of God's Church, the especial meditation, and recommendation of this Psalm. And under a third obligation too, that it is one of those five Psalms, the daily rehearsing whereof, is enjoined to me, by the constitutions of this Church, as five other are to every other person of our body. As the whole book is manna, so these five Psalms are my gomer, which I am to fill and empty every day of this manna.

Now as the spirit and soul of the whole Book of Psalms is contracted into this Psalm, so is the spirit and soul of this whole Psalm contracted into this verse.

10. CHRIST'S TREATMENT OF THE SUPPLIANT

Matt. 9. 2: "Jesus seeing their faith said unto the sick of the palsy; Son, be of good cheer; thy sins be forgiven thee."

Where we see first, our Saviour Christ opening the bowels of compassion to him, and receiving him so, as if he had issued out of his bowels, and from his loins, in that gracious appellation, *Fili, My son*. He does not call him brother; for greater enmity can be no where, than is often expressed to have been between brethren; for in that degree, and distance, enmity amongst men began in Cain and Abel, and was pursued in many pairs of brethren after, in sacred and in secular story. He does not call him friend; that name, even in Christ's own mouth, is not always accompanied with good entertainment; *Amice, quomodo intrasti*, says he, *Friend, how came you in? and he bound him hand and foot and cast him into outer darkness*. He does not call him son of Abraham, which might give him an interest in all the promises, but he gives him a present adoption, and so a present fruition of all, *Fili, My son*. His son, and not his son-in-law; he loads him not with the encumbrances, and half-impossibilities of the law, but he seals to him the whole Gospel, in the remission of sins. His son, and not his disinherited son, as the Jews were, but his son, upon whom he settled his ancient inheritance, his eternal election, and his new purchase, which he came now into the world to make with his blood. His son, and not his prodigal son, to whom Christ imputes no wastefulness of his former graces, but gives him a general release, and *quietus est*, in the forgiveness of sins. All that Christ asks of his sons, is, *Fili da mihi cor, My son give me thy heart*; and till God give us that, we cannot give it him; and therefore in this son he creates a new heart, he infuses a new courage, he establishes a new confidence, in the next word, *Fili confide, My son be of good cheer*.

Christ then does not stay so long wrestling with this man's faith, and shaking it, and trying whether it were fast rooted, as he did with that woman in the Gospel, who came after him, in her daughter's behalf, crying, *Have mercy upon me, O Lord, thou Son of David*, for Christ gave not that woman one word; when her importunity made his disciples speak to him, he said no more, but that he was not sent to such as she; this was far, very far from a *Confide, filia, Daughter, be of good cheer;* but yet, this put her not off, but (as it follows) *She followed, and worshipped him, and said, O Lord help me*: and all this prevailed no farther with him, but to give such an answer, as was more discomfortable than a silence, *It is not fit to take the children's bread, and cast it unto dogs*. She denies not that, she contradicts him not; she says, *Truth Lord*, it is not fit to take the children's bread to cast it unto dogs, and *Truth Lord*, I am one of those dogs; but yet she perseveres in her holy importunity, and in her good ill-manners, and says, *Yet the dogs eat of the crumbs which fall from their master's table*: and then, and

28

not till then comes Jesus to that, *O woman, great is thy faith, be it unto thee, even as thou wilt: and her daughter was healed.*

But all this, at last, was but a bodily restitution, here was no *dimittuntur peccata* in the case, no declaration of forgiveness of sins: but with this man in our text, Christ goes farther, and comes sooner to an end; he exercises him with no disputation, he leaves no room for any diffidence, but at first word establishes him, and then builds upon him.

Now beloved, which way soever of these two God have taken with thee, whether the longer, or the shorter way, bless thou the Lord, praise him, and magnify him for that. If God hath settled and strengthened thy faith early, early in thy youth heretofore, early at the beginning of a sermon now, a day is as a thousand years with God, a minute is as six thousand years with God, that which God hath not done upon the nations, upon the Gentiles, in six thousand years, never since the Creation, which is, to reduce them to the knowledge and application of the Messiah, Christ Jesus, that he hath done upon thee, in an instant. If he have carried thee about the longer way, if he have exposed thee to scruples, and perplexities, and storms in thine understanding, or conscience, yet in the midst of the tempest, the soft air, that he is said to come in, shall breathe into thee; in the midst of those clouds, his Son shall shine upon thee; in the midst of that flood he shall put out his rainbow, his seal that thou shalt not drown, his sacrament of fair weather to come, and as it was to the thief, thy cross shall be thine altar, and thy faith shall be thy sacrifice. Whether he accomplish his work upon thee soon or late, he shall never leave thee all the way, without this *Confide fili*, a holy confidence, that thou art his, which shall carry to the *dimittuntur peccata*, to the peace of conscience, in the remission of sins.

11. CATHOLICITY SEEN IN THE CALL-
ING OF THE APOSTLES

Matt. 4. 18, 19: "Jesus, walking by the sea of Galilee, saw two brethren, Simon called Peter, and Andrew his brother, casting a net into the sea: for they were fishers. And he saith unto them, Follow me, and I will make you fishers of men."

These persons . . . our Saviour Christ calls to him, and he called them by couples, by pairs; two together. So he called his creatures into the world at the first creation, by pairs. So he called them into the ark, for the reparation of the world, by pairs, two and two. God loves not singularity; the very name of Church implies company; it is *concio*, *congretatio*, *coetus*; it is a congregation, a meeting, an assembly; it is not in any one man; neither can the Church be preserved in one man. And therefore it hath been dangerously said (though they confess it to have been said by many of their greatest divines in the Roman Church), that during the time that our blessed Saviour lay dead in the grave, there was no faith left upon the earth, but only in the Virgin Mary; for then there was no Church. God hath manifested his will in two Testaments; and though he have abridged and contracted the doctrine of both in a narrow room, yet he hath digested it into two commandments, *Love God, love thy neighbour*. There is but one Church; that is true, but one; but that Church cannot be in any one man; there is but one baptism; that is also true, but one; but no man can baptize himself; there must be *sacerdos et competens* (as our old canons speak); a person to receive, and a priest to give baptism. There is but one faith in the remission of sins; that is true too, but one; but no man can absolve himself; there must be a priest and a penitent. God calls no man so, but that he calls him to the knowledge, that he hath called more than him to that Church, or else it is an illusory, and imaginary calling, and a dream.

Take heed therefore of being seduced to that Church that is in one man; *in scrinio pectoris*, where all infallibility, and assured resolution is in the breast of one man; who (as their own authors say) is not bound to ask the counsel of others before, nor to follow their counsel after. And since the Church cannot be in one, in an unity, take heed of bringing it too near that unity, to a paucity, to a few, to a separation, to a conventicle. The Church loves the name of Catholic; and it is a glorious, and an harmonious name; love thou those things wherein she is Catholic, and wherein she is harmonious, that is, *Quod ubique*, *quod semper*, those universal, and fundamental doctrines, which in all Christian ages, and in all Christian Churches, have been agreed by all to be necessary to salvation; and then thou art a true Catholic. Otherwise, that is, without relation to this Catholic and universal doctrine, to call a particular Church Catholic (that she should be Catholic, that is, universal in dominion, but not in doctrine) is such a solecism, as to speak of a white blackness, or a great littleness; a particular Church to be universal implies such a contradiction.

Christ loves not singularity; he called not one alone; he loves not schism neither between them whom he calls: and therefore he calls persons likely to agree, two brethren (*He saw two brethren, Peter and Andrew, etc.*). So he began to build the synagogues, to establish that first government, in Moses and Aaron, brethren; so he begins to build the Church, in Peter and Andrew, brethren.

12. ON PRAYER

(a) Wandering Thoughts in Prayer

When we consider with a religious seriousness the manifold weaknesses of the strongest devotions in time of prayer, it is a sad consideration. I throw myself down in my chamber, and I call in and invite God and his angels thither, and when they are there, I neglect God and his angels for the noise of a fly, for the rattling of a coach, for the whining of a door; I talk on, in the same posture of praying; eyes lifted up; knees bowed down; as though I prayed to God; and, if God or his angels should ask me when I thought last of God in that prayer, I cannot tell; sometimes I find that I had forgot what I was about, but when I began to forget it, I cannot tell. A memory of yesterday's pleasures, a fear of to-morrow's dangers, a straw under my knee, a noise in mine ear, a light in mine eye, an any thing, a nothing, a fancy, a chimera in my brain, troubles me in my prayer. So certainly is there nothing, nothing in spiritual things, perfect in this world.

(b) Unconscious Prayer

That soul that is accustomed to direct herself to God upon every occasion, that, as a flower at sun-rising, conceives a sense of God in every beam of his, and spreads and dilates itself towards him in a thankfulness, in every small blessing that he sheds upon her; that soul that, as a flower at the sun's declining, contracts and gathers in and shuts up herself as though she had received a blow, whensoever she hears her Saviour wounded by an oath or blasphemy or execration; that soul who, whatsoever string be struck in her, bass or treble, her high or her low estate, is ever tuned towards God, that soul prays sometimes when it does not know that it prays.

13. EARTH'S CREATION AND DISSOLUTION

Gen. 1. 26: "And God said, Let us make man in our image, after our likeness."

Never such a frame, so soon set up, as this, in this chapter. For, for the thing itself, there is no other thing to compare it with. For it is all, it is the whole world. And for the time, there was no other time to compare it with, for this was the beginning of time, *In the beginning God created heaven and earth.*

The earth which in some thousands of years men could not look over, nor discern what form it had (for neither Lactantius, almost three hundred years after Christ, nor St Augustine, more than one hundred years after him, would believe the earth to be round); that earth which no man in his person is ever said to have compassed till our age; that earth which is too much for man yet (for, as yet, a very great part of the earth is unpeopled); that earth which, if we will cast it all but into a map, costs many months' labour to grave it, nay, if we will cast but a piece of an acre of it into a garden, costs many years' labour to fashion and furnish it; all that earth, and then that heaven which spreads so far as that subtle men have with some appearance of probability imagined that in that heaven, in those manifold spheres of the planets and the stars, there are many earths, many worlds, as big as this which we inhabit; that earth and that heaven which spent God himself, Almighty God, six days in furnishing; Moses sets up in a few syllables, in one line, *in principio*, in the beginning God created heaven and earth.

If a Livy or a Guicciardine, or such extensive and voluminous authors, had had this story in hand, God must have made another world, to have made them a library to hold their books of the making of this world. Into what wire would they have drawn out this earth? Into what leaf-gold would they have beat out these heavens?

It may assist our conjecture herein to consider that amongst those men, who proceed with a sober modesty and limitation in their writing, and make a conscience not to clog the world with unnecessary books, yet the volumes which are written by them, upon this beginning of Genesis, are scarce less than infinite. God did no more but say, Let this and this be done; and Moses does no more but say that upon God's saying it was done. God required not nature to help him to do it; Moses required not reason to help him to be believed. The Holy Ghost hovered upon the waters, and so God wrought: the Holy Ghost hovered upon Moses too, and so he wrote. And we believe these things to be so, by the same Spirit in Moses' mouth, by which they were made so in God's hand.

Only, beloved, remember that a frame may be thrown down in a much less time than it was set up. A child, an ape, can give fire to a cannon; and a vapour can shake the earth; and these fires, and these vapours, can throw down cities in minutes. When Christ said, Throw down this temple, and in three days I will raise it, they never stopped upon the consideration of throwing it down; they knew that might soon be done; but they wondered at the speedy raising of it.

Now, if all this earth were made in that minute, may not all come to a speedy dissolution in this minute? Or may not thy acres, thy miles, thy shires, shrink into feet, and so few feet as shall but make up thy grave? When he who was a great lord, must be but a cottager; and not so well, for a cottager must have so many acres to his cottage; but in this case, a little piece of an acre, five-foot, is become the house itself; the house, and the land; the grave is all. Lower than that; the grave is the land, and the tenement, and the tenant too; he that lies in it becomes the same earth that he lies in. They all make but one earth, and but a little of it.

But then raise thyself to a higher hope again. God hath made better land, the land of promise; a stronger city, the new Jerusalem; and inhabitants for that everlasting city, us; whom he made, not by saying, Let there be men, but by consultation, by deliberation, God said, *Let us make man in our own image, after our likeness.*

14. BELIEF IN THE CHURCH

There is . . . a whole bundle of those things, which we are bound to pray for, in the Lord's Prayer; and *fasciculus credendorum*, a whole bundle of those things, which we are bound to believe in the Apostles' Creed; and in that last bundle of myrrh, in that Creed, is this particular, *ut credamus hoc*, that we believe this, this, that God hath established means of salvation here, and *he that believeth not this*, that such a commission there is, *shall be damned*.

In that bundle of myrrh then, where lies this that must necessarily be believed, this commission? In that article of the Creed, *Credo ecclesiam Catholicam*, *I believe the holy Catholic Church*; for till I come to that grain of myrrh, to believe the Catholic Church, I have not the savour of life; let me take in the first grain of this bundle of myrrh, the first article, *Credo in Deum Patrem*, *I believe in God the Father*. By that I have a being, I am a creature, but so is a contemptible worm, and so is a venomous spider as well as I, so is a stinking weed, and so is a stinging-nettle, as well as I; so is the earth itself that we tread under our feet, and so is the ambitious spirit, which would have been as high as God, and is lower than the lowest, the devil himself is a creature as well as I; I am but that, by the first article, but a creature; and I were better, if I were not that. But take a great deal of this myrrh together, consider more articles, that Christ is conceived, and born, and crucified, and dead, and buried, and risen, and ascended, there is some savour in this; but yet, if when we shall come to judgement, I must carry into his presence, a menstruous conscience, and an ugly face, in which his image, by which he should know me, is utterly defaced, all this myrrh of his merits, and his mercies, is but a savour of death unto death unto me, since I, that knew the horror of my own guiltiness, must know too, that whatsoever he be to others, he is a just Judge, and therefore a condemning Judge to me. If I get farther than this in the Creed, to the *Credo in Spiritum sanctum*, *I believe in the Holy Ghost*, where shall I find the Holy Ghost? I lock my door to myself, and I throw myself down in the presence of my God, I divest myself of all worldly thoughts, and I bend all my powers and faculties upon God, as I think, and suddenly I find myself scattered, melted, fallen into vain thoughts, into no thoughts; I am upon my knees, and I talk, and think nothing; I deprehend myself in it, and I go about to mend it, I gather new forces, new purposes to try again, and do better, and I do the same thing again. *I believe in the Holy Ghost*, but do not find him, if I seek him only in private prayer; but *in ecclesia*, when I go to meet him in the Church, when I seek him where he hath promised to be found, when I seek him in the execution of that commission, which is proposed to our faith in this text, in his ordinances, and means of salvation in his Church, instantly the savour of this myrrh is exalted, and multiplied to me; not a dew, but a shower is poured out upon me, and presently follows *Communio Sanctorum*, *the Communion of Saints*, the assistance of militant and triumphant Church in my behalf; and presently follows *Remissio peccatorum, the Remission of sins*, the purifying of my conscience, in that water, which is his blood, baptism, and in that wine, which is his blood, the other sacrament; and presently follows *carnis Resurrectio, a Resurrection of my body*; my body becomes no burthen to me; my body is better now, than my soul was before; and even here I have Goshen in my Egypt, incorruption in the midst of my dunghill, spirit in the midst of my flesh, Heaven upon earth; and presently follows *vita aeterna, life everlasting*; this life of my body shall not last for ever, nay the life of my soul in Heaven is not such as it is at the first. For that soul there, even in Heaven, shall receive an addition, an access of joy, and glory in the resurrection of our bodies in the consummation.

When a wind brings the river to any low part of the bank, instantly it overflows the whole meadow; when that wind which blows where he will, the Holy Ghost, leads an humble soul to the article of the Church to lay hold upon God, as God hath exhibited himself in his ordinances, instantly he is surrounded under the blood of Christ Jesus, and all the benefits thereof, *the Communion of Saints, the Remission of sins, the Resurrection of the body, and the life everlasting*, are poured out upon him.

15. GOD'S LOVING DISCIPLINE

Let me wither and wear out mine age in a discomfortable, in an unwholesome, in a penurious prison, and so pay my debts with my bones, and recompense the wastefulness of my youth with the beggary of mine age: Let me wither in a spital under sharp, and foul, and infamous diseases, and so recompense the wantonness of my youth, with that loathsomeness in mine age; yet, if God withdraw not his spiritual blessings, his Grace, his patience, if I can call my suffering his doing, my passion his action, all this that is temporal is but a caterpillar got into one corner of my garden, but a mildew fallen upon one acre of my corn; the body of all, the substance of all is safe, as long as the soul is safe.

But when I shall trust to that, which we call a good spirit, and God shall deject, and impoverish, and evacuate that spirit; when I shall rely upon a moral constancy, and God shall shake, and enfeeble, and enervate, destroy and demolish that constancy; when I shall think to refresh myself in the serenity and sweet air of a good conscience, and God shall call up the damps and vapours of hell itself, and spread a cloud of diffidence, and an impenetrable crust of desperation upon my conscience; when health shall fly from me, and I shall lay hold upon riches to succour me, and comfort me in my sickness, and riches shall fly from me, and I shall snatch after favour, and good opinion, to comfort me in my poverty; when even this good opinion shall leave me, and calumnies and misinformations shall prevail against me; when I shall need peace, because there is none but thou, O Lord, that should stand for me, and then shall find, that all the wounds that I have, come from thy hand, all the arrows that stick in me, from thy quiver; when I shall see that because I have given myself to my corrupt nature, thou hast changed thine; and because I am all evil towards thee, therefore thou hast given over being good towards me; when it comes to this height, that the fever is not in the humours, but in the spirits, that mine enemy is not an imaginary enemy, fortune, nor a transitory enemy, malice in great persons, but a real, and an irresistible, and an inexorable, and an everlasting enemy, the Lord of Hosts himself, the Almighty God himself, the Almighty God himself only knows the weight of this affliction, and except he put in that *pondus gloriae*, that exceeding weight of an eternal glory, with his own hand, into the other scale, we are weighed down, we are swallowed up, irreparably, irrevocably, irrecoverably, irremediably.

16. CHRIST'S WILLING SURRENDER
TO THE CROSS

Ps. 68: "Unto God the Lord belong the issues of death."[1]

Be now content to consider with me how to this *God the Lord belonged the issues of death.* That God, the Lord, the Lord of life could die, is a strange contemplation; that the Red Sea could be dry, that the sun could stand still, that an oven could be seven times heat and not burn, that lions could be hungry and not bite, is strange, miraculously strange, but supermiraculous that God could die; but that God would die is an exaltation of that. But even of that also it is a superexaltation, that God should die, must die, and *non exitus* (saith St Augustine), God the Lord had no issue but by death, and *oportuit pati* (saith Christ himself), "all this Christ ought to suffer", was bound to suffer; *Deus ultionum Deus*, saith David, God is the "God of revenges", he would not pass over the sin of man unrevenged, unpunished. But then *Deus ultionum libere egit* (says that place), The God of revenges works freely, he punishes, he spares whom he will. And would he not spare himself? He would not: *Dilectio fortis ut mors*, "love is as strong as death", stronger, it drew in death that naturally was not not welcome. *Si possibile*, saith Christ, "if it be possible, let this cup pass", when his love expressed in a former decree with his Father had made it impossible. "Many

[1] I.e., from death.

44

waters quench not love"; Christ tried many; he was baptized out of his love, and his love determined not[1] there, he wept over Jerusalem out of his love, and his love determined not there. He mingled blood with water in his agony, and that determined not his love; he wept pure blood, all his blood at all his eyes, at all his pores, in his flagellation and thorns (to the Lord our God belonged the issues of blood), and these expressed, but these did not quench his love.

He would not spare, nay he would not spare himself. There was nothing more free, more voluntary, more spontaneous than the death of Christ. 'Tis true, *libere egit*, he died voluntarily, but yet when we consider the contract that had passed between his Father and him, there was an *oportuit*, a kind of necessity upon him. All this Christ ought to suffer. . . .

His Father calls it but a bruise, and but a bruising of his heel ("The serpent shall bruise his heel") and yet that was, that the serpent should practise and compass his death. Himself calls it but a baptism, as though he were to be the better for it. "I have a baptism to be baptized with", and he was in pain till it was accomplished, and yet this baptism was his death. The Holy Ghost calls it joy ("For the joy that was set before him he endured the cross") which was not a joy of his reward after his passion but a joy that filled him even in the midst of those torments, and arose from them; when Christ calls his passion *Calicem* a cup, and no worse ("Can ye drink of my Cup?") he speaks not odiously, not with detestation

[1] I.e., ended not.

of it. Indeed it was a cup, *salus mundo*, a health to all the world. And *quid retribuam*, says David, "What shall I render unto the Lord?" Answer you with David, *accipiam Calicem*, "I will take the cup of salvation", take that, that cup is salvation, his passion, if not into your present imitation, yet into your present contemplation.

And behold how that Lord that was God, yet could die, would die, must die, for your salvation. That Moses and Elias talked with Christ in the Transfiguration both St Matthew and St Mark tell us, but what they talked of, only St Luke. *Dicebant excessum ejus*, says he, they talked of his decease, of his death which was to be accomplished at Jerusalem. The word is of his exodus, the very word of our text, *exitus*, his issue by death.

Moses, who in his *Exodus* had prefigured this issue of our Lord, and in passing Israel out of Egypt through the Red Sea, had foretold in that actual prophecy Christ passing of mankind through the sea of his blood. And Elias, whose exodus and issue out of this world was a figure of Christ's ascension, had no doubt a great satisfaction in talking with our blessed Lord *de excessu ejus*, of the full consummation of all this in his death, which was to be accomplished at Jerusalem.

Our meditation of his death should be more visceral and affect us more because it is of a thing already done.

17. A CONCEPTION OF HELL AS THE LOSS OF GOD

When all is done, the hell of hells, the torment of torments is the everlasting absence of God, and the everlasting impossibility of returning to his presence; *Horrendum est*, says the Apostle, *It is a fearful thing to fall into the hands of the living God* . . . but to fall out of the hands of the living God, is a horror beyond our expression, beyond our imagination.

That God should let my soul fall out of his hand, into a bottomless pit, and roll an unremovable stone upon it, and leave it to that which it finds there (and it shall find that there, which it never imagined, till it came thither), and never think more of that soul, never have more to do with it. That of that providence of God, that studies the life of every weed, and worm, and ant, and spider, and toad, and viper, there should never, never, any beam flow out upon me; that that God, who looked upon me when I was nothing, and called me when I was not, as though I had been, out of the womb and depth of darkness, will not look upon me now, when, though a miserable, and a banished, and a damned creature, yet I am his creature still, and contribute something to his glory, even in my damnation; that that God, who hath often looked upon me in my foulest uncleanness, and when I had shut out the eye of the day, the sun, and the eye of the night, the taper, and the eyes of all the world with curtains and windows, and doors, did yet see me, and see me in mercy, by making me see that he saw me, and sometimes brought me to a present remorse, and (for that time) to a forbearing of that sin, should so turn himself from me, to his glorious saints and angels, as that no saint nor angel, nor Christ Jesus himself, should ever pray him to look towards me, never remember him that such a soul there is ... that that God should frustrate all his own purposes and practices upon me, and leave me, and cast me away, as though I had cost him nothing, that this God at last, should let this soul go away, as a smoke, as a vapour, as a bubble, and that then this soul cannot be a smoke, a vapour, nor a bubble, but must lie in darkness, as long as the Lord of light is light itself, and never spark of that light reach to my soul. What Tophet is not paradise, what brimstone is not amber, what gnashing is not a comfort, what gnawing of the worm is not a tickling, what torment is not a marriage bed to this damnation, to be secluded eternally, eternally, eternally, from the sight of God?

18. ON FREQUENT COMMUNION

In the primitive Church, there was an erroneous opinion of such an absolute necessity in taking this sacrament, as that they gave it to persons when they were dead; a custom which was grown so common, as that it needed a canon of a council to restrain it. But the giving of this sacrament to children newly baptized was so general, even in pure times, as that we see so great men as Cyprian and Augustine, scarce less than vehement for the use of it; and some learned men in the reformed Church have not so far declined it, but that they call it *Catholicam consuetudinem*, a Catholic, an universal custom of the Church. But there is a far greater strength both of natural and spiritual faculties required for the receiving of this Sacrament of the Lord's Supper, than the other of baptism. But for those who have those faculties, that they are now, or now should be able, to discern the Lord's body, and their own souls, besides that inestimable and inexpressible comfort, which a worthy receiver receives, as often as he receives that seal of his reconciliation to God, since as baptism is *tessera Christianorum* (I know a Christian from a Turk by that sacrament), so this sacrament is *tessera orthodoxorum* (I know a Protestant from a Papist by this sacrament), it is a service to God and to his Church to come frequently to this communion; for truly (not to shake or affright any tender conscience) I scarce see how any man can satisfy himself that he hath said the Lord's Prayer with a good conscience, if at the same time he were not in such a disposition as that he might have received the sacrament too; for, if he be in charity, he might receive, and if he be not, he mocked Almighty God, and deluded the congregation, in saying the Lord's Prayer.

19. THE LIBERALITY OF THE HOLY GHOST

That liberality which was, in the former acceptation, but a relieving, but a refreshing, but a repairing of defects and dilapidations in the body or fortune, is now, in this second part, in this spiritual acceptation, the raising of a dejected spirit, the redintegration of a broken heart, the resuscitation of a buried soul, the reconsolidation of a scattered conscience—not with the glues and cements of this world, mirth and music, and comedies and conversations, and wine and women (miserable comforters are they all), nor with that meteor that hangs between two worlds, that is, philosophy and moral constancy (which is somewhat above the carnal man, but yet far below the man truly Christian and religious). But this is the liberality of which the Holy Ghost himself is content to be the steward, of the holy, blessed, and glorious Trinity, and to be notified, and qualified by that distinctive notion, and specification, *The Comforter.*

To find a languishing wretch in a sordid corner, not only in a penurious fortune, but in an oppressed conscience, his eyes under a diverse suffocation, smothered with smoke, and smothered with tears, his ears estranged from all salutation, and visits, and all sounds, but his own sighs and the storms and thunders and earthquakes of his own despair, to enable this man to open his eyes, and see that Christ Jesus stands before him, and says, *Behold and see, if ever there were any sorrow, like my sorrow*, and my sorrow is overcome, why not is thine? To open this man's ears, and make him hear that voice that says, *I was dead, and am alive, and behold, I live for evermore, Amen*; and so mayest thou; to bow down those heavens, and bring them into his sad chamber. To set Christ Jesus before him, to out-sigh him, out-weep him, out-bleed him, out-die him. To transfer all the fasts, all the scorns, all the scourges, all the nails, all the spears of Christ Jesus upon him, and so, making him the crucified man in the sight of the Father, because all the actions, and passions of the Son, are appropriated to him, and made his so entirely, as if there were never a soul created but his. To enrich this poor soul . . . so, as that he shall believe, and by believing find all Christ to be his, this is that liberality which we speak of now, in dispensing whereof, *The liberal man deviseth liberal things, and by liberal things shall stand.*

20. HEAVENLY JOY BEGINS ON EARTH

If you look upon this world in a map, you find two hemispheres, two half worlds. If you crush Heaven into a map, you will find two hemispheres too, two half heavens; half will be joy, and half will be glory; for in these two, the joy of Heaven, and the glory of Heaven is all Heaven often represented unto us. And as of those two hemispheres of the world, the first hath been known long before, but the other (that of America, which is the richer in treasure) God reserved for later discoveries; so though he reserve that hemisphere of Heaven which is the glory thereof, to the resurrection, yet the other hemisphere, the joy of Heaven, God opens to our discovery, and delivers for our habitation even whilst we dwell in this world.

As God hath cast upon the unrepentant sinner two deaths, a temporal and a spiritual death, so hath he breathed into us two lives; for so, as the word for death is doubled, *Morte morieris, Thou shalt die the death*, so is the word for life expressed in the plural, *Chaiim, vitarum, God breathed into his nostrils the breath of lives*, of divers lives.

Though our natural life were no life, but rather a continual dying, yet we have two lives besides that, an eternal life reserved for Heaven, but yet a heavenly life too, a spiritual life, even in this world; and as God doth thus inflict two deaths, and infuse two lives, so doth he also pass two judgements upon man, or rather repeats the same judgement twice. For that which Christ shall say to thy soul then at the Last Judgement, *Enter into thy Master's joy*, he says to thy conscience now, *Enter into thy Master's joy*. The everlastingness of the joy is the blessedness of the next life, but the entering, the inchoation, is afforded here. . . .

Howling is the noise of hell, singing the voice of Heaven; sadness the damp of hell, rejoicing the serenity of Heaven. And he that hath not this joy here lacks one of the best pieces of his evidence for the joys of Heaven; and hath neglected or refused that earnest by which God uses to bind his bargain, that true joy in this world shall flow into the joy of Heaven as a river flows into the sea. This joy shall not be put out in death, and a new joy kindled in me in Heaven; but as my soul, as soon as it is out of my body, is in Heaven, and does not stay for the possession of Heaven, nor for the fruition of the sight of God, till it be ascended through air, and fire, and moon, and sun, and planets, and firmament, to that place which we conceive to be Heaven, but without the thousandth part of a minute's stop, as soon as it issues, is in a glorious light, which is Heaven (for all the way to Heaven is Heaven; and as those angels which came from Heaven hither bring Heaven with them, and are in Heaven here, so that soul that goes to Heaven meets Heaven here; and as those angels do not divest Heaven by coming, so these souls invest Heaven in their going).

As my soul shall not go towards Heaven, but go by Heaven to Heaven, to the Heaven of Heavens, so the true joy of a good soul in this world is the very joy of

Heaven; and we go thither, not that being without joy we might have joy infused into us, but that as Christ says, *Our joy might be full*, perfected, sealed with an everlastingness; for, as he promises, *That no man shall take our joy from us*, so neither shall death itself take it away, nor so much as interrupt it or discontinue it; but as in the face of death, when he lays hold upon me, and in the face of the devil when he attempts me, I shall see the face of God (for every thing shall be a glass to reflect God upon me), so in the agonies of death, in the anguish of that dissolution, in the sorrows of that valediction, in the irreversibleness of that transmigration, I shall have a joy which shall no more evaporate than my soul shall evaporate—a joy that shall pass up and put on a more glorious garment above, and be joy superinvested in glory. *Amen.*

21. IMMORTALITY AND RESURRECTION

Christ establishes a resurrection, a resurrection there shall be, for that makes up God's circle. The body of man was the first point that the foot of God's compass was upon: first, he created the body of Adam: and then he carries his compass round, and shuts up where he began, he ends with the body of man again in the glorification thereof in the resurrection. God is Alpha and Omega, first and last; and his alpha and omega, his first and last, work is the body of man too. Of the immortality of the soul, there is not an express article of the creed: for that last article of *the life everlasting*, is rather *de praemio*, *et poena*, what the soul shall suffer, or what the soul shall enjoy, being presumed to be immortal than that it is said to be immortal in that article; that article may, and does presuppose an immortality, but it does not constitute an immortality in our soul, for there would be life everlasting in Heaven, and we were bound to believe it, as we were bound to believe a God in Heaven, though our souls were not immortal.

There are so many evidences of the immortality of the soul, even to a man's natural reason, that it required not an article of the creed, to fix this notion of the immortality of the soul. But the resurrection of the body is discernible by no other light but that of faith, nor could be fixed by any less assurance than an article of the creed.

Where be all the splinters of that bone, which a shot hath shivered and scattered in the air? Where be all the atoms of that flesh, which a corrosive hath eat away, or a consumption hath breathed, and exhaled away from our arms and other limbs? In what wrinkle, in what furrow, in what bowel of the earth, lie all the grains of the ashes of a body burnt a thousand years since? In what corner, in what ventricle of the sea lies all the jelly of a body drowned in the general flood? What coherence, what sympathy, what dependence maintains any relation, any correspondence, between the arm which was lost in Europe, and that leg that was lost in Africa or Asia scores of years between?

One humour of our dead body produces worms, and those worms suck and exhaust all other humour, and then all dies, and all dries and moulders into dust, and that dust is blown into the river, and that puddled water tumbled into the sea, and that ebbs and flows in infinite revolutions, and still, still God knows in what cabinet every seed-pearl lies, in what part of the world every grain of every man's dust lies; and *sibilat populum suum* (as his prophet speaks in another case (Zech. 10. 8)) he whispers, he hisses, he beckons for the bodies of his saints, and in the twinkling of an eye, that body that was scattered over all the elements, is sat down at the right hand of God, in a glorious resurrection. A dropsy hath extended me to an enormous corpulency and unwieldiness; a consumption hath attenuated me to a feeble macilency and leanness, and God raises me a body such as it should have been, if these infirmities had not intervened and deformed it.

David could go no further in his book of Psalms, but

to that, *Let every thing that hath breath praise the Lord*;
Ye, says he, ye that have breath, praise ye the Lord, and
that ends the book: but, that my dead body should come
to praise the Lord, this is that new song which I shall
learn and sing in Heaven; when not only *my soul* shall
magnify the Lord, and *my spirit rejoice in God my Saviour*;
but shall I have mine old eyes, and ears, and tongue, and
knees, and receive such glory in my body myself as that,
in that body, so glorified by God, I also shall glorify
him.

22. THE SOUL'S MARRIAGE TO CHRIST

Christ hath married my soul: and he hath married it *in aeternum*, for ever, which is the third and last circumstance in this spiritual, as it was in the secular marriage.

And here the *aeternum* is enlarged; in the secular marriage it was an eternity considered only in this life ; but this eternity is not begun in this world, but from all eternity in the Book of Life, in God's eternal decree for my election, there Christ was married to my soul. Christ was never in minority,[1] never under years; there was never any time when he was not as ancient as the ancient of days, as old as his Father. But when my soul was in a strange minority, infinite millions of millions of generations, before my soul was a soul, did Christ marry my soul in his eternal decree. So it was eternal, it had no beginning. Neither doth he interrupt this by giving me any occasion of jealousy by the way, but loves my soul as though there were no other soul, and would have done and suffered all that he did for me alone, if there had been no name but mine in the Book of Life.

And as he hath married me to him, *in aeternum*, for ever, before all beginnings, and *in aeternum*, for ever, without any interruptions, so I know, that *whom he loves he loves to the end*, and that he hath given me, not a presumptuous impossibility, but a modest infallibility, that

---

[1] Was Donne's mind harking back here to the secret marriage in which, wedding Ann More, a minor, he broke Canon Law, and suffered imprisonment and separation from her for many months?

no sin of mine shall divorce or separate me from him; for that which ends the secular marriage ends not the spiritual: not death, for my death does not take me from that husband, but that husband being by his Father preferred to higher titles, and greater glory in another state, I do but go by death where he is become a king, to have my part in that glory and in those additions which he hath received there. And this hath led to our third and last marriage, our eternal marriage in the triumphant Church.

And in this third marriage, the persons are the Lamb and my soul; *The marriage of the Lamb is come, and blessed are they that are called to the marriage supper of the Lamb,* says St John, speaking of our state in the general resurrection. That Lamb that was brought to *the slaughter and opened not his mouth,* and I who have opened my mouth and poured out imprecations and curses upon men, and execrations and blasphemies against God upon every occasion; that Lamb who *was slain from the beginning,* and was slain by him who *was a murderer from the beginning;* that *Lamb which took away the sins of the world,* and I who brought more sins into the world, than any sacrifice but the blood of this Lamb could take away: this Lamb and I (these are the persons) shall meet and marry; there is the action.

This is not a clandestine marriage, not the private seal of Christ in the obsignation of his Spirit; and yet such a clandestine marriage is a good marriage: nor it is not such a parish marriage, as when Christ married me to himself at my baptism, in a church here; and yet that marriage of a Christian soul to Christ in that sacrament is a blessed marriage: but this is a marriage in that great and glorious congregation, where all my sins shall be laid open to the eyes of all the world, where all the blessed virgins shall see all my uncleanness, and all the martyrs see all my tergiversations, and all the confessors see all my double dealings in God's cause; where Abraham shall see my faithlessness in God's promises; and Job my impatience in God's corrections; and Lazarus my hardness of heart in distributing God's blessings to the poor; and those virgins, and martyrs, and confessors, and Abraham, and Job, and Lazarus, and all that congregation shall look upon the Lamb and upon me and upon one another as though they would all forbid those banns, and say to one another, Will this Lamb have any thing to do with this soul? And yet there and then this Lamb shall marry me, *in aeternum,* for ever, which is our last circumstance.

It is not well done to call it a circumstance, for the eternity is a great part of the essence of that marriage. Consider then how poor and needy a thing all the riches of this world, how flat and tasteless a thing all the pleasures of this world, how pallid and faint and dilute a thing all the honours of this world are, when the very treasure and joy and glory of Heaven itself were imperfect if it were not eternal, and my marriage shall be too *in aeternum,* for ever.

23. YEARNING FOR THE HOUSE OF GOD

Ps. 63. 2, 3: "My soul thirsteth for thee, my flesh also longeth after thee: in a barren and dry land where no water is. Thus have I looked for thee in holiness, that I might behold thy power and glory."

Was this David's case? Was he fallen thus far, into a diffidence in God? No. But the danger, the precipice, the slippery sliding into that bottomless depth, is, to be excluded from the means of coming to God, or staying with God; and this is that that David laments here, that by being banished and driven into the wilderness of Judah, he had not access to the sanctuary of the Lord, to sacrifice his part in the praise, and to receive his part in the prayers of the congregation; for angels pass not to ends, but by ways and means, nor men to the glory of the triumphant Church, but by participation of the communion of the militant.

To this note David sets his harp, in many, many psalms: sometimes, that God had suffered his enemies to possess his tabernacle (*He forsook the tabernacle of Shiloh, he delivered his strength into captivity, and his glory into the enemies' hands*)[1], but most commonly he complains that God disabled him from coming to the sanctuary. In which one thing he had summed up all his desires, all

[1] It is noticeable that here and often in his sermon quotations of the Psalms Donne does not give our Prayer Book version, since the Authorized Version of the Psalms was still used in the Church's worship.

his prayers (*One thing have I desired of the Lord, that I will look after; that . . . I may dwell in the house of the Lord, all the days of my life, to behold the beauty of the Lord, and to inquire in his temple*). His vehement desire of this he expresses again, *My soul thirsteth for God, for the living God; when shall I come and appear before God?* He expresses a holy jealousy, a religious envy, even to the sparrows and swallows, yea, *the sparrow hath found her a house, and the swallow a nest for herself, and where she may lay her young, even thine altars, O Lord of hosts, my King and my God*. Thou art my King and my God, and yet excludest me from that which thou affordest to sparrows, *And are we not of more value than many sparrows?*

And as though David felt some false-ease, some half-temptation, some whispering that way, that God is *in the wilderness Judah*, in every place as well as in his *Sanctuary*, there is in the original in that place a pathetical, a vehement, a broken expressing expressed, *O thine altars*. It is true (says David) thou art here in the wilderness, and I may see thee here, and serve thee here, but, *O thine altars, O Lord of hosts, my King and my God!* When David could not come in person to that place, yet he bent towards the temple (*In thy fear will I worship towards thy holy temple*). Which was also Daniel's devotion: when he prayed, *his chamber windows were open towards Jerusalem*: and so is Hezekiah's turning to the wall to weep, and to pray in his sick bed, understood to be to that purpose, to conform, and compose himself towards the temple. In the place consecrated for that use,

God by Moses fixes the service, and fixes the reward: and towards that place (when they could not come to it) doth Solomon direct their devotion in the consecration of the temple (*When they are in the wars, when they are in captivity, and pray towards this house, do thou hear them*). For, as in private prayer, when (according to Christ's command) we are shut in our chamber, there is exercised *modestia fidei*, the modesty and bashfulness of our faith, not pressing upon God in his house: so in the public prayers of the congregation, there is exercised the fervour and holy courage of our faith, for *Agmine facto obsidemus Deum*, it is a mustering of our forces, and a besieging of God.

Therefore does David so much magnify their blessedness that are in this house of God (*Blessed are they that dwell in thy house, for they will be still praising thee*), those that look towards it may praise thee sometimes, but those men who dwell in the Church, and whose whole service lies in the Church, have certainly an advantage of all other men (who are necessarily withdrawn by worldly businesses) in making themselves acceptable to Almighty God, if they do their duties, and observe their church services aright.

Man being therefore thus subject naturally to manifold calamities, and spiritual calamities being incomparably heavier than temporal, and the greatest danger of falling into such spiritual calamities being in our absence from God's house, where only the outward means of happiness are ministered unto us, certainly there is much tenderness and deliberation to be used, before the church doors be shut against any man.

Now of those divers gates which God opens in this life, those divers exercises of charity, the particular which we are occasioned to speak of here [i.e., Gen. 28. 16, 17] is not the clothing, nor feeding of Christ, but the housing of him, the providing Christ a house, a dwelling; whether this were the very place where Solomon's temple was after built, is perplexedly, and perchance impertinently, controverted by many; but howsoever, here was the house of God, and here was the gate of Heaven. It is true, God may be devoutly worshipped anywhere; *In omni loco dominationis ejus benedic anima mea Domino*; In all places of his dominion, my soul shall praise the Lord, says David.

It is not only a concurring of men, a meeting of so many bodies, that makes a church; if thy soul and body be met together, an humble preparation of the mind, and a reverent disposition of the body, if thy knees be bent to the earth, thy hands and eyes lifted up to Heaven, if thy tongue pray and praise, and thine ears hearken to his answer, if all thy senses and powers and faculties be met with one unanime purpose to worship thy God, thou art, to this intendment, a church, thou art a congregation, here are two or three met together in his name, and he is in the midst of them, though thou be alone in thy chamber. The Church of God should be built upon a rock, and yet Job had his church upon a dunghill; the bed is a scene and an emblem of wantonness, and yet Hezekiah had his church in his bed; the Church is to be placed upon the top of a hill, and yet the prophet Jeremy had his church *in luto*, in a miry dungeon; constancy and settledness belongs to the Church, and yet Jonah had his church in the whale's belly; the lion that roars and seeks whom he may devour, is an enemy to this Church, and yet Daniel had his church in the lion's den; *aquae quietudinum*, the waters of rest in the Psalm, where a figure of the Church, and yet the three children had their church in the fiery furnace; liberty and life appertain to the Church, and yet Peter and Paul had their church in prison, and the thief had his church upon the cross. Every particular man is himself *templum Spiritus sancti*, a temple of the Holy Ghost; yea, *solvite templum hoc*, destroy this body by death and corruption in the grave, and yet there shall be *festum encaeniorum*, a renewing, a re-edifying of all those temples in the general resurrection: when we shall rise again, not only as so many Christians, but as so many Christian Churches to glorify the apostle and high priest of our profession, Christ Jesus, in that eternal Sabbath. *In omni loco dominationis ejus*, Every person, every place is fit to glorify God in.

25. HOW TO LISTEN TO SERMONS

It is the glory of God's word, not that it is come, but that it shall remain for ever: it is the glory of a Christian, not that he hath heard, but that he desires to hear still. Are the angels weary of looking upon that face of God which they looked upon yesterday? Or are the saints weary of singing that song which they sung to God's glory yesterday? And is not that Hallelujah, that song which is their morning and evening sacrifice, and which shall be their song world without end, called still *a new song*?

Be not you weary of hearing those things which you have heard from others before: do not say, if I had known this, I would not have come, for I have heard all this before; since thou never thoughtest of it since that former hearing, till thou heardest it again now, thou didst not know that thou hadst heard it before. . . .

If then God hath placed thee under such a pastor as presents thee variety, bless God who enlarges himself to afford thee that spiritual delight in that variety; even for the satisfaction of that holy curiosity of thine. If he have placed thee under one who often repeats, and often remembers thee of the same things, bless God even for that, that in that he hath let thee see that the Christian religion is *verbum abbreviatum*, a contracted doctrine, and that they are but a few things which are necessary to salvation, and therefore be not loath to hear them often.

Our errand hither, then, is not to see; but much less not to be able to see, to sleep: it is not to talk, but much less to snort: it is to hear, and to hear all the words of the preacher, but to hear in those words the word, that word which is the soul of all that is said, and is the true physic of all their souls that hear. . . .

The word of God is made a sermon, that is, a text is dilated, diffused into a sermon; but that whole sermon is not the word of God. But yet all the sermon is the ordinance of God. *Delight thyself in the Lord, and he will give thee thy heart's desire*; take a delight in God's ordinance, in man's preaching, and thou wilt find God's word in that. . . . When the pleasant words of God's servants have conveyed the saving word of God himself into thy soul, then mayest thou say with Christ to the spouse, *I have eaten my honeycomb with my honey* (Cant. 5. 1), mine understanding is enlightened with the words of the preacher, and my faith is strengthened with the word of God; I glorify God much in the gifts of the man, but I glorify God much more in the gifts of his grace; I am glad I have heard him, but I am gladder I have heard God in him; I am happy that I have heard those words, but thrice happy that in those words I have heard the word; blessed be thou that camest in the name of the Lord, but blessed be the Lord that is come to me in thee; let me remember how the preacher said it, but let me remember rather what he said.

And beloved, all the best of us all, all that all together, all the days of our life, shall be able to say unto you is but this, that if ye will hear the same Jesus in the same gospel by the same ordinance, and not seek an imaginary Jesus in an illusory sacrifice in another Church, if you will hear so as you have contracted with God in your baptism, the Holy Ghost shall fall upon you whilst you hear, here in the house of God, and the Holy Ghost shall accompany you home to your own houses and make your domestic peace there, a type of your union with God in Heaven; and make your eating and drinking there a type of the abundance and fullness of Heaven; and make every day's rising to you there a type of your joyful resurrection to Heaven; and every night's rest a type of your eternal Sabbath; and your very dreams, prayers and meditations and sacrifices to Almighty God.

26. THE COMFORT OF THE HOLY SPIRIT

When those days were come, that the *Bridegroom was to be taken from them*, Christ Jesus to be removed from their personal sight and conversation, and therefore even the *children of the marriage chamber were to mourn and fast*; when that Church that mourned, and lamented his absence, when she was but his *spouse*, must necessarily mourn now in a more vehement manner, when she was to be (in some sense) his *widow*; when that *shepherd* was not only to be *smitten*, and so *the flock dispersed* (this was done in his passion), but he was to be taken away in his ascension; what a powerful comforter had that need to be that should be able to recompense the absence of Christ Jesus himself, and to infuse comfort into his orphans, the children of his marriage chamber, into his widow, the desolate and disconsolate Church, into his flock, his amazed, his distressed and (as we may, properly enough, say in this case) his beheaded apostles and disciples? *Quantus ergo Deus, qui dat Deum?*

Less than God could not minister this comfort; how great a God is he that sends a God to comfort us? And how powerful a comforter he, who is not only sent by God, but is God?

Therefore does the Apostle enlarge and dilate, and delight his soul upon this comfort, *Blessed be God, even the Father of our Lord Jesus Christ, the Father of mercies, and the God of all comfort, who comforteth us in all our tribulations, that we may be able to comfort them which are in any affliction, by that comfort wherewith ourselves are comforted of God.*

The Apostle was loath to depart from the word *comfort*; and therefore, as *God, because he could swear by no greater, sware by himself,* so, because there is no stronger adjuration, than the comfort itself, to move you to accept this comfort as the Apostle did, so we intreat you by that, *If there be any consolation in Christ, if any comfort of love, if any fellowship of the Spirit, if any bowels and mercy,* Lay hold upon this true comfort, the coming of the Holy Ghost, and say to all the deceitful comforts of this world, not only *Vane consolati estis,* Your comforts are frivolous, but *Onerosi consolatores,* Your comforts are burdensome; there is not only a disappointing of hope, but an aggravating of sin, in entertaining the comforts of this world. As Barnabas, that is, *Filius consolationis, The Son of consolation,* that he might be capable of this comfort, divested himself of all worldly possessions. . . .

Heaven is glory, and Heaven is joy; we cannot tell which most; we cannot separate them; and this comfort is joy in the Holy Ghost. This makes all Job's states alike; as rich in the first chapter of his book, where all is suddenly lost, as in the last, where all is abundantly restored.

This consolation from the Holy Ghost makes my midnight noon, mine executioner a physician, a stake and pile of faggots, a bonfire of triumph. This consolation makes a satire and slander and libel against me a panegyric and an elogy in my praise; it makes a *tolle* an *ave,* a *vae* an *euge,* a *crucifige* an *Hosanna,* it makes my death-bed a marriage bed, and my passing-bell an epithalamium.

27. THE SIN OF SPOILING CHILDREN

How infinite, and how miserable a circle of sin do we make, if as we sinned in our parent's loins before we were born, so we sin in our children's actions when we are dead, by having given them either example or liberty of sinning. We have a fearful commination from God upon a good man, upon Eli, for his not restraining the licentiousness of his sons; *I will do a thing in Israel*, says God there, *at which every man's ears that hears it shall tingle;* and it was executed, Eli fell down, and broke his neck.

We have also a consolation to women for children, *She shall be saved in child-bearing*, says the Apostle; but as Chrysostom and others of the ancients observe and interpret that place (which interpretation arises out of the very letter) it is, *si permanserint*, not if she, but if they, if the children continue in faith, in charity, in holiness and sobriety. The salvation of the parents hath so much relation to the children's goodness, as that if they be ill by the parent's example or indulgence, the parents are as guilty as the children.

Art thou afraid thy child should be stung with a snake, and wilt thou let him play with the old serpent, in opening himself to all temptations? Art thou afraid to let him walk in an ill air, and art thou content to let him stand in that pestilent air that is made of nothing but oaths and execrations of blasphemous mouths round about him?

28. PREACH THE GOSPEL BY LIVING IT

He that says well, presents a good text, but he that lives well presents a good comment upon that text. As the best texts that we can take, to make sermons upon, are as this text is, some of the words of Christ's own sermons, so the best arguments we can prove our sermons by is our own life. The whole week's conversation is a good paraphrase upon the Sunday's sermon; it is too soon to ask when the clock struck eleven, is it a good preacher? For I have but half his sermon then, his own life is the other half; and it is time enough to ask the Saturday after, whether the Sunday's preacher preach well or no; for he preaches poorly that makes an end of his sermon upon Sunday. He preaches on all the week, if he live well, to the edifying of others. If we say well, and do ill, we are so far from the example of God's children which built with one hand and fought with the other, as that if we do build with one hand in our preaching, we pull down with the other in our example, and not only our own, but other men's buildings too. For the ill life of particular men reflects upon the function and ministry in general.

And as it is with us, if we divorce our words and our works, so it is with you, if you do divorce your faith and your works.

JOHN HALES (1584–1656)

Hales was one of the best-known scholars of his time, and in 1612 was made Professor of Greek at Oxford, where in the following year he preached the funeral oration for Sir Thomas Bodley.

In 1618 James I sent him, as a moderate Calvinist, with three other divines, to represent the English Church at the Synod of Dort. Here, however, he quickly shed his Calvinism—"There", he said, "I bid John Calvin Good Night."

He became Fellow of Eton, and later Laud appointed him to a prebend at Windsor. He belonged to the little group of quiet thinkers who eschewed controversy, and were wont to assemble for discussion at Great Tew, Lord Falkland's mansion. Hales himself believed (a view rather of a retired student than of a practical theologian) that all Christians might be persuaded to join in a liturgy which excluded controversial statement.

However, he refused to sign the Covenant, and, being deprived of his Fellowship, fell into poverty, and was obliged to sell his library.

His dislike of controversy is seen in the prayer, printed below (Extract 31), which he delivered at the end of a sermon upon "Peace I leave unto you, my peace I give unto you."

Universally loved and respected, he was characteristically described in the last year of his life by John Audrey as "a prettie little man, sanguine and of a cheerfull countenance, very gentile and courteous".

In 1659 his works were published in *The Golden Remains of the ever-memorable Mr John Hales*.

29. THE ENTICING SWEETNESS OF GOD'S INSTRUCTION

One thing by the providence of God our nature hath, which makes this rough way to learn more plain and easy: it is φιλόμυθος. Common experience shows we are all very desirous to hear narrations and reports, either pleasant or strange; wise men therefore, and God which is wiser than men, being to train up mankind, *genus indicile*, a subject dull of hearing, and hardly drawn to learn, have from time to time wrought upon this humour, upon this part of our disposition, and mitigated, sugared, as it were, the unpleasantness of a difficult and hard lesson with the sweetness of some delightful parable or fable. And St Chrysostom tells us of a physician who, finding his patient to abhor physic but infinitely long for wine, heating an earthen cup in the fire, and quenching it in wine, put his potion therein, that so the sick person being deceived with the smell of wine, might unawares drink of the physic: or, that I may better draw my comparison from Scripture, as when Jacob meant to be welcome to his father Isaac, he put on his brother Esau's apparel, and so got access. So, beloved, wise men, when they meant either to instruct the ignorant, or to reprove offenders, to procure their welcome, and make their way more passable, have been wont for the most part, as it were, to clothe their lesson or reproof in a parable, or to serve it in a dish savouring of wine, so that Jacob might be admitted under Esau's coat, that the smell of the

pleasantness of wine might draw down the wholesome-
ness of physic.

Great and singular have been those effects, which this
kind of teaching by parables hath wrought in men; by
informing their ignorance, reproving their error, working
patience of reproof; opening the understanding, moving
the affections, and other such commodities, ου μόνον οἱ
ποίηται, ἀλλὰ καὶ πόλεις, κὰι νομοθέται τοῦ χρησίμου χάριν
τοὺς μύθους ἀνεδέξαντο. And for this cause not only our
poets and profane authors, but whole cities, and men
that gave laws to commonwealths, have made especial
choice of this course.

Yea, our Saviour Christ himself hath filled the Gospels
with parables, made them like a divine and Christian
Æsop's Fables, because he found it to be exceeding
profitable. For, first of all, it is the plainest and most
familiar way, and above all other stoops to the capacity
of the learner, as being drawn from either trees, or beasts,
or from some ordinary common and known actions of
men; as from a shepherd attending his flock, from an
husbandman sowing corn in his field, from a fisher casting
his net into the sea, from a woman putting leaven into
her dough, or the like. So that in this respect a parable is
like Moses' Tabernacle, which outwardly was nothing
but goat-skins or some ordinary stuff, but within it was
silk, and purple, and gold.

30. THE NEED OF PERPETUAL PRAYER

Devotion in ordinary persons is a thing easily raised, and easily allayed. Every strange event, every fear, every little calamity or distress is enough to put us into a strain of religious meditation; but on the contrary side, a small matter doth again as quickly kill it. It seems to be like a quotidian ague, it comes by fits, every day it takes us, and every day it leaves us: or like flax, or straw, or such light and dry stuff, which easily kindles, and as soon goes out. Indeed, it is a good thing when we find our hearts thus tender, and upon every occasion ready to melt into devotion: for as to be quick of sense is a sign of life, and the purest and best complexions are quickest of sense, so it is a great argument of spiritual life in us, and of purity of soul, when we are εὐόλισθοι, so easily apt to fall upon devout meditation.

But our Saviour requires yet another quality in our devotion: it must be as lasting as it is quick. Quintilian advises his orator to beware how he stand too long upon a place of passion, because that passion is not lasting, *et nihil facilius lachrymis marcescit*, and men cannot long weep. But, beloved, our Saviour gives other precepts of Christian oratory; he wills, if we will prevail with God, to insist and dwell long upon a place of religious passion, and provide that our tears may be perpetual and never dry: an hard thing you will take it to be, yet certainly it is very possible.

There is a question raised among the great masters of

natural learning, Whether or no there may be a lamp so provided that it may burn for ever? And they think it may be done. Beloved, our Saviour here teaches to practise that in spirituals, which hath been but a matter of speculation in naturals, even so to kindle and dress our lamps that they shall never go out; but be like unto the good housewife's candle in the Proverbs, that goes not out by night, or rather like the sun which shines for evermore. Daniel is said to have kindled this lamp, and to have made his prayer thrice a day, David seven times a day, but this is not enough; for in that the one is noted to have prayed seven times a day, the other thrice, it is likely at other times they did not pray, but God is not contented with this intermittent prayer; for if we look upon my text,[1] we shall see that there must be no instant free from prayer: we must not measure our prayers by number. . . . That that measures out our prayer must be line and length, some continued quantity, whose parts have no separation, no intermission: for so saith my text, "men ought always to pray". Always, the whole life of a man ought to be but one continual prayer.

But let us a little consider how possible this is, and see if there be anything that doth necessarily enforce intermission of prayer. And first, that wonderful lamp of which I but now told you great scholars had spoken, is not yet made, because they are not agreed of what matter to make it. And indeed in the world, things either are not at all, or being do at length cease to be, either because

[1] Luke 18. 1: "And he spake a parable unto them to this end, that men ought always to pray, and not to faint."

there is no fit matter whence they may be framed, or else the matter of which they are made vanishes and dies.

But, beloved, prayer is a strange thing, it can never want matter: it will be made Αναξαγορικῶς, *e quo libet*, out of any matter, upon any occasion whatsoever; whatsoever you do, wheresoever you are, doth minister occasion of some kind of prayer; either of thanksgiving unto God for his goodness; or of praising and admiring his greatness; or of petitioning to him in case of want or distress; or bewailing some sin, or neglect committed. Is it the consideration of God's benefits that will move us to thankfulness? Then certainly our thankfulness ought to be perpetual, there is no person so mean, no soul so poor, and distressed, and miserable, but if he search narrowly, he shall find some blessing, for which he owes thankfulness unto God. If nothing else, yet his very misery and distress is a singular blessing, if he use it to that end for which it was sent. Is it the consideration of distress and affliction, and some degree of the curse of God upon us, that will stir our devotion? Indeed this is it with most men that kindles the fire of prayer in our hearts. Men for the most part are like unto the unslaked lime, which never heats till you throw water upon it; so they never grow warm in devotion, till somewhat contrary to their wishes and disposition begins to afflict them: then certainly our petitions to God ought never to cease. For never was there man in any moment of his life entirely happy, either in body, goods, or good name: every man hath some part of affliction.

Blessing and cursing, though they seem to be enemies,

and contrary one to another, yet are never severed, but go hand in hand together. Some men have more of one, some of another, but there is no man but hath some part of both; wherefore as it seems not only prayer in general, but all kind, all sort of prayer ought to be continual. Prayer must not be, as it were, of one thread; we must blend and temper together all kind of prayer, our praise or thanks, our sorrow, and make our prayer like Joseph's particoloured coat, like a beautiful garment of sundry colours.

So then, as fire goes not out so long as it hath matter to feed on, so what shall be able to interrupt our devotion which hath so great and everlasting store of matter to continue it?

31. PRAYER FOR PEACE IN THE CHURCH

When our friends and enemies do both jointly consent to lay open our shame, to whose judgement shall we appeal, or whither shall we fly? Whither? Even to thee, O Lord Christ; but not as to a judge: too well we know thy sentence. Thou hast sent us messengers of peace, but we, like Jerusalem, thy ancient love, have not understood the things belonging to our peace. O Lord, let us know them in this our day, and let them no longer be hidden from our eyes. Look down, O Lord, upon thy poor dismembered Church, rent and torn with discords, and even ready to sink. Why should the neutral or atheist any longer confirm himself in his irreligion by reasons drawn from our dissensions? Or why should any greedy-minded worldling prophesy unto himself the ruins of thy sanctuary, or hope one day to dip his foot in the blood of thy Church? We will hope, O Lord (for what hinders?) that notwithstanding all supposed impossibilities, thou wilt one day in mercy look down upon thy Sion, and grant a gracious interview of friends so long divided. Thou that wroughtest that great reconciliation between God and man, is thine arm waxen shorter? Was it possible to reconcile God to man? To reconcile man to man is it impossible? Be with those, we beseech thee, to whom the persecution of Church controversies is committed, and, like a good Lazarus, drop one cooling drop into their tongues and pens, too, too much exasperated each against other. And if it be thy determinate will and counsel that this abomination of desolation, standing where it ought not, continue unto the end, accomplish thou with speed the number of thine elect, and hasten the coming of thy Son our Saviour, that he may himself in person sit and judge, and give an end to our controversies, since it stands not with any human possibility. Direct thy Church, O Lord, in all her petitions for peace, teach her wherein her peace consists, and warn her from the world, and bring her home to thee; that all those that love thy peace may at last have the reward of the sons of peace, and reign with thee in thy kingdom of peace for ever. Grant this, O God, for thy Son's sake, Jesus Christ our Lord, to whom with thee and the Holy Ghost be ascribed all praise, might, majesty, and dominion, now and for ever.

HENRY HAMMOND (1605–60)

Henry Hammond (who must not be confused with William Hammond the poet) has been named for his erudite Biblical studies "the father of English Biblical Criticism". He aimed in his preaching to avoid controversial subjects, and to induce his hearers to study Scripture more eagerly.

Dr W. H. Hutton has described his sermons as "models of the best Caroline prose in its simplicity, restraint, clarity, distinction . . . In his absence of conceits, he shows himself typically a Caroline rather than an Elizabethan". The later Carolines preferred a simple style to oratory.

A reader would therefore look in vain in Hammond's sermons for the quips of Andrewes, the golden eloquence of Jeremy Taylor, or the grandeur of Donne. Hammond was content to preach of charity, toleration, and Christian conduct rather than of the great splendours of theological thought and fact.

Very characteristic of his sermons is one on "Have any of the Pharisees believed on him?", in which he pointed out that established learning—whether it be of the Pharisees, or of Mohammedanism in the time of the Crusades, or of Romanism by Protestantism —is not easily overcome by new thought. For true Christian living there is great need of a learning deeply versed in the *abscondita Domini Dei nostri*—the Incarnation and the Atonement. Such learning will not inculcate habitual hostility to others, but rather a wide charity.

In the extract, here given, of another sermon he urges that the St Matthew account of the Last Judgement should stir us to more frequent acts of mercy, physical and spiritual.

32. CHRISTIAN ACTS OF MERCY

If the story of Christ coming to judgement, set down in the 25th of Matthew after the 30th verse, had ever entered through the doors of our ears to the inward closets of our hearts, it is impossible but we should observe and practise that one single duty there required of us. Christ there as a Judge exacts and calls us to account for nothing in the world but only works of mercy, and according to the satisfaction which we are able to give him in that one point he either entertains or repels us; and therefore our care and negligence in this one business will prove us either Christians or infidels.

But, alas! it is too plain that in our actions we never dream either of the judgement or the arraignment; our stupid neglect of this one duty argues us not only unchristian but unnatural.

Besides our almsdeeds, which concern only the outside of our neighbour and are but a kind of worldly mercy, there are many more important but cheaper works of mercy, as good counsel, spiritual instructions, holy education of them that are come out of our loins, or are committed to our care, seasonable reproof, according to that excellent place, "Thou shalt not hate thy brother in thine heart, but in any wise reprove him": a care of carrying ourselves that we may not scandal, or injure, or offer violence to the soul and tender conscience of him that is flexible to follow us into any riot.

These and many other works of mercy in the highest

degree, as concerning the welfare of other men's souls, and the chief thing required of us at the day of judgement, are yet so outdated in our thoughts, so utterly defaced and blotted out in the whole course of our lives, that it seems we never expect that Christ in his majesty as a Judge, whom we apprehend and embrace and hug in his humility as a Saviour.

Beloved, till by some severe hand held over our lives, and particularly by the daily study and exercise of some work of mercy or other, we demonstrate the sincerity of our belief, the saints on earth and angels in Heaven will shrewdly suspect that we do only say over that part of our creed, that we believe only that which is for our turn, the sufferings and satisfactions of Christ which cost us nothing, but do not proceed to his office of a Judge, do not either fear his judgements, or desire to make ourselves capable of his mercies.

Briefly, whosoever neglects or takes no notice of this duty of exercising works of mercy, whatsoever he brags of in his theory or speculation, in his heart either denies or contemns Christ as Judge, and so destroys the sum of his faith; and this is another kind of secret atheism.

MARK FRANK (1613-64)

Frank was a Fellow of Pembroke Hall, Cambridge, when in 1643, soon after the execution of Laud, the Puritan Earl of Manchester, with his two chaplains, visited the leading "Malignants" of Cambridge University, and bade them, under pain of dismissal from Cambridge and their college labours within three days, to sign the Solemn League and Covenant. Mark Frank, with the Master of Pembroke, and many other devout and learned men, chose exile and poverty.

At the Restoration Frank was restored to his Fellowship (and, a little later, to the Mastership) at Pembroke, becoming also in succession Archdeacon of St Albans, and Treasurer and Prebendary of St Paul's Cathedral.

As a preacher he stands mid-way between the "witty" preachers, with their successors Donne and Jeremy Taylor, and the simpler preachers with homelier style leading up to Tillotson. Eschewing over-lengthy sentences and quotations, he did this so successfully, yet eloquently, that Dr W. F. Mitchell in his *English Pulpit Oratory from Andrewes to Tillotson* hails him as "the fairest star in the constellation of the 'witty' preachers". But his "wit" was not too complicated to be intelligible to the common man.

Though shorter than those of Donne or Jeremy Taylor, each of his sermons has material—vivid, imaginative, scriptural, Catholic—for two or three modern sermons.

33. ANNUNCIATION B.V.M. [I]
THE FITNESS OF THE MESSENGER

Luke 1. 28: "The angel came in unto her, and said, Hail, thou that art highly favoured, the Lord is with thee: blessed art thou among women."

Dominus mecum, and *Dominus tecum* too, the Lord be with me whilst I am speaking it, and with you whilst you are hearing it, and bless us both whilst we are about it, that we may learn to bless where we should bless, whom, and when, and how to do it, and rightly both accept and apply God's blessings and our own.

We are now to learn it from the angel, his visiting and blessing the blessed Virgin here. . . .

And who (1) so fit as an angel to come in to her—to give this visit—to give this blessing? It was a bad angel that brought the curse upon the woman—it was fit a good one should bring the blessing.

The employment (2) suits none so well. It was news of joy; who could bring it better than one of those who were the first sons of eternal joy—the first enjoyers of it—who could pronounce it better?

Who better (3) to come with a *Dominus tecum*, before the face of the Lord, with a message of his coming down to earth, than they who always behold his face in Heaven?

Who fitter (4) to come to her? She was an immaculate and unspotted virgin; and to whom do virgins' chambers lie open at midnight but to angels? God sends no other thither at that time of night; and that that time it was may well be conjectured from Wisdom 18. 14, 15: "When all things were in quiet silence, and that night was in the midst of her swift course, thine almighty Word came down from heaven"; then, it seems, was the time of her conception, of Christ's coming to her; before whom immediately the angel came to bear the message that he was a-coming, if, as St Bernard says, he were not come already.

And (5) with such a message to a virgin, as that she should conceive without a man, who was convenient to bring it but an angel? *Ne quo degenere depravaret affectu*, says St Ambrose, that there might not be the least ground of a false suspicion.

But (6) to such a virgin, one so highly favoured as to be made the mother of God (for the mother of Christ is no less, he being God) what messenger could come less than an angel? Prophets and patriarchs were too little for so great an embassage, and angels never came upon a greater.

Nay (7) every angel neither was not fit for so high an office. The Angel Gabriel it was—he is the ὁ ἄγγελος here. Gabriel is by St Jerome and St Gregory interpreted *fortitudo Dei*—the power or strength of God; and in this work it appeared indeed; God's strength and power never so much shown as in the saving of us by Christ. It is by others interpreted *vir Deus* or *Deus nobiscum*—God man, or God with us. Could any be thought fitter to bring this news upon his lips, than he that carries it in his name? Especially, being the same that foretold all this to Daniel,

—fit that he should see to the performance who brought the promise. Petrus Damiani thinks he was the holy Virgin's guardian angel—proper therefore to bring her this good message, or any else. God had several times employed him before, to Daniel, Zacharias, and others, and found him faithful; he therefore now employs him still, that we may know, he that is faithful in the least, God will by degrees trust him with the most, the greatest matters.

34. ANNUNCIATION B.V.M. [II]
THE HONOUR DUE TO OUR LADY

Blessed art thou among Women

Give we her in God's name the honour due to her. God hath styled her "blessed" by the angel, by Elizabeth; commanded all generations to call her so, and they hitherto have done it, and let us do it too. Indeed, some of late have overdone it; yet let us not therefore underdo it, but do it as we hear the angel and the first Christians did it; account of her and speak of her as the most blessed among women, one "highly favoured", most "highly" too. But all the while give *Dominus tecum*, all the glory, the whole glory of all to him; give her the honour and blessedness of the chief of saints—him only the glory that she is so, and that by her conceiving and bringing our Saviour into the world we are made heirs, and shall one day be partakers of the blessedness she enjoys, when the Lord shall be with us too, and we need no angel at all to tell us so.

"Blessed", blessed of God, blessed of men; blessed in the city, and blessed in the field. Cities and countries call her blessed; blessed in the fruit of her body, in her blessed child Jesus. Blessed in the fruit of her ground, her cattle, her kine, and her sheep, in the inferior faculties of her soul and body; all fructify to Christ. Blessed her basket and her store, her womb and her breasts; the womb that bare him and the paps that gave him suck.

Blessed in her going out and in her coming in, the Lord still being with her; the good treasure of heaven still open to her, showering down upon her, and the earth filled with the blessings which she brought into the world when she brought forth the Son of God. Blessed she indeed that was the conduit of so great blessings, though blessed most in the bearing him in her soul, much more than bearing him in her body. So Christ indicates to the woman that began to "bless the womb", that is, the mother "that bare him"; "Yea, rather", says he, "they that hear the word of God and keep it"; as if he had said, She is more blessed in bearing the Word in her soul than in her body. But blessed she is; Elizabeth, by the Holy Spirit fell a-blessing her when she came to see her; and she herself by the same Spirit tells us "all generations shall call me blessed". So we have sufficient example and authority to do it. And I hope we will not suffer the Scripture to speak false, but do it.

The second ground of blessedness is in the text too. *Dominus tecum*, the Lord's being with her. From Christ's being with her and with us it is that we are blessed. From his Incarnation begins the date of all our happiness. If God be not with us all the world cannot make us happy, much less blessed. From this grace of the Incarnation first riseth all our glory; so that, "Not unto us, O Lord, not unto us, but unto thy name give the praise", must she sing as well as we; and they do her wrong as well as God, that give his glory unto her, who will not give his glory to another, though to his mother, because she is but his earthly mother,—a thing infinitely distant from the heavenly Father. Nor would that humble handmaid, if she should understand the vain and fond, and almost idolatrous styles and honours that are given her somewhere upon earth, be pleased with them; she is highly favoured enough that her Lord and Son is with her and she with him; she would be no higher sharer.

35. CATHOLIC MANNERS

Luke 1. 28: "The angel came in unto her, and said, Hail, thou that art highly favoured, the Lord is with thee: blessed art thou among women."

Good words, if it be no more, are fittest, sure, for Christian mouths; but yet good wishes too; for he that forbids to say to some, "God speed you", intimates we should say so to others; and though the disciples are bid to "salute no man by the way"—that is, when it will retard or hinder their holy business—they are yet bid, when they come into a house, say "Peace be to it". And if the angel do it, and Christ bid it, and do it too, as he does, I hope we may and will do too; nay, and give good titles too, upon the same account: the angel does so to the blessed Virgin; and we hasten to them. "Thou that art highly favoured", blessed, "blessed among women".

"Thou that art highly favoured"; but why "thou" without a name? Why not Mary here as well as after? Why? There he used her name to dispel her fear, as it were, by a kind of friendly familiarity; here he forbears it in his reverence to her. We use not to salute great persons by their names, but by their titles; and the Mother of God is above the greatest we here meet with upon the earth. We must not be too familiar with those whom God so highly favours; that is our lesson hence. We are not to speak of the blessed Virgin, the Apostles, and Saints, as if we were speaking to our servants, Paul, Peter, Mary, or the like. It is a new fashion of religion, neither taken from saints, nor angels, nor any of Heaven or heavenly spirits, to unsaint the saints, to deny them their proper titles, to level them with the meanest of our servants. We might learn better manners from the angel here— manners, I say, if it were nothing else; for we dare not speak so to any here who are above us, and we think much to be *thoued*, without our titles, by that new generation of possessed men, who yet with more reason may call the best man thou, than we the Apostles John or Thomas.

36. THE SWADDLING-CLOTHES OF
THE NATIVITY

Luke 2. 7: "And she brought forth her firstborn son, and wrapped him in swaddling-clothes, and laid him in a manger; because there was no room for them in the inn."

The clothes his dear mother wrapped him in are the very badges of humility; σπάργανον is a rag, or torn and tattered clothes: such were the clothes she wrapped him in—such, he is so humble, he will be content with, even with rags. What make we then such ado for clothes? Jacob would bargain with God no further than for raiment to put on: he covenanted with him not for fashion, nor colour, nor stuff, nor trimming: and our blessed Lord here is content with what comes next. But, Lord! to see what ado have we about our apparel! this lace, and that trimming; this fashion, and that colour; these jewels, and those accoutrements; this cloth, and that stuff; this silk, and that velvet; this silver, and that gold; this way of wearing, and that garb in them; as if our whole life were raiment, our clothes heaven, and our salvation the handsome wearing them. We forget, we forget our sweet Saviour's rags, his poor ragged swaddling-clothes; and our garments witness against us to our faces, our pride, our follies, our vanities at the best. . . .

Well, but though he was content to be wrapped in swaddling-clothes, and those none of the handsomest, neither, may we not look for a cradle at least to lay him in? No matter what we may look for, we are like to find no better than a manger for that purpose, and a lock of hay for his bed, and for his pillow, and for his mantle too. A poor condition, and an humble one indeed, for him whose chariot is the clouds, whose palace is in Heaven, whose throne is with the Most High. What place can we hereafter think too mean for any of us? Stand thou here, sit thou there, under my foot-stool—places of exceeding honour compared to this. What, not a room among men, not among the meanest, in some smoky cottage, or ragged cell; but among beasts? Whither hath thy humility driven thee, O Saviour of mankind? Why, mere pity of a woman in thy mother's case, O Lord, would have made the most obdurate have removed her from the horses' feet, the asses' heels, the company of unruly beasts, from the ordure and nastiness of a stable. . . .

What though there be no room for him in the inn? I hope there is in our houses for him. It is Christmas time, and let us keep open house for him; let his rags be our Christmas raiment, his manger our Christmas cheer, his stable our Christmas great chamber, hall, dining-room. We must clothe with him, and feed with him, and lodge with him at this feast. He is now ready by and by to give himself to eat; you may see him wrapped ready in the swaddling-clothes of his blessed sacrament; you may behold him laid upon the altar as in his manger. Do but make room for him, and we will bring him forth, and you shall look upon him, and handle him, and feed upon him: bring we only the rags of a rent and torn and broken and contrite heart, the white linen cloths of pure intentions and honest affections to swathe him in, wrap him up fast, and lay him close to our souls and bosoms. It is a day of mysteries: it is a mysterious business we are about; Christ wrapped up, Christ in the sacrament, Christ in a mystery; let us be content to let it go so, believe, admire, and adore it. It is sufficient that we know Christ's swaddling-clothes: his righteousness will keep us warmer than all our winter garments; his rags hold out more storms than our thickest clothes: let us put them on. His manger feeds us better than all the Asian delicates, all the dainties of the world; let us feed our souls upon him. His stable is not hanged here with arras, or decked with gilded furniture; but it is hung infinitely with gifts and graces: the stable is dark, but there is the Light of the world to enlighten it. . . .

Thy poverty, O sweet Jesu, shall be my patrimony, thy weakness my strength, thy rags my riches, thy manger my kingdom; all the dainties of the world, but chaff to me in comparison of thee; and all the room in the world, no room to that, wheresoever it is, that thou vouchsafest to be. Heaven it is wheresoever thou stayest or abidest; and I will change all the house and wealth I have for thy rags and manger.

37. WELCOMING THE MESSIAH

Matt. 21. 9: "And the multitudes that went before, and that followed, cried, saying, Hosanna to the Son of David: Blessed is he that cometh in the Name of the Lord; Hosanna in the highest."

The multitudes before are, in the mystery, the holy patriarchs, and they that followed are the prophets. Now what the patriarchs and prophets have rejoiced at, that must we. Abraham says, Christ himself "rejoiced to see my day, he saw it and was glad". Yes, your father Abraham was glad. He was glad to see Christ a-coming. The prophets are everywhere full of joyful expressions at the mention of the Messiah's coming; their eyes looked, and their hearts longed for him; and the prophet Zachary calls to us to tell it out with joy to the daughter of Sion, tells punctually even of this very joy and coming too. And "what was written beforetime", either by patriarch or prophet, "was written for our learning", says the Apostle. We may do what they did, what they would have us.

Or, the multitudes before in the mystery are the Jews; the multitudes that follow are the Gentiles. Both bidden by the Apostle to rejoice, "Rejoice, ye Gentiles, with his people": his people, the Jews, before, and the Gentiles behind, all shall rejoice in his salvation: for glory is now coming to the Jews, glory to his people Israel, and light unto the Gentiles, to light them by his coming. So sang old Simeon in his song.

The multitudes before is the Jewish synagogue; the multitudes behind, the Christian Church; a multitude, indeed, that cannot be numbered, of emperors, and kings, and princes; bishops and priests; doctors, martyrs, confessors, and virgins, all in their several orders and generations, crying, "Hosanna to the Son of David", the "whole world gone after him". Before, indeed, only *Notus in Judaea Deus*, God only known in Jewry; his coming only talked of in Israel; but, after, *Quam admirabile nomen tuum in universa terra!* "O Lord our Governor, how wonderful (or excellent) is thy name in all the world!" All these multitudes—the Jew, with his multitude of patriarchs, priests, and Levites, and singers, and prophets, with his sacrifices of bulls, and rams, and goats, and sheep, of types and figures, all crying out Messiah is coming;—the Christians, apostles, martyrs, confessors, doctors, virgins, bishops, priests, and deacons, and all several orders in their choirs and churches throughout the world, crying out, He is come; all the corners of the earth resounding out Hosannas and Allelujahs to him. *Una est fides praecedentium atque sequentium populorum*, says St Gregory; all believing and professing the same he that cometh here; they, the Jews, before, crying "He that cometh"; we, the Christians, crying "He that is come", or rather, He that cometh still, that every day comes to us by his grace, and through his word, and in his sacraments: "Blessed is he that cometh" still, not a tense or tittle changed; he that comes being the same for ever; eternity and things eternal being ever coming, never gone or going.

So now the congregation is full, what should we do but begin our service? when we have Law, and Prophets, and Gospel to countenance and bear us company in our Te Deum and Benedictus, at our prayers and praises, in our joys and festivals; all of them crying nothing but Christ, nothing but Christ, blessed be he, blessed be he, and blessed be his coming, and blessed be his day, and blessed be his deeds; the whole practice of all Christian churches and congregations that ever were gathered together *in nomine Domini*, "in the name of the Lord", till these mere nominal verbal Christians, that are afraid of the name of him that cometh, of the name of Jesus, of blessing it or bowing at it; all Christians, all that came before in the name of Christ, till these pretenders that follow nobody but their own fancies; all agreeing in the same welcome to their Redeemer, joining in the same prayers and praises: what should we do but add our voices and sing with them?

38. FASTING

1 Cor. 9. 27: "But I keep under my body, and bring it
into subjection . . . "

Nor is it so hard a business as men would seem to make
it: none of all the ways I told you of for the subduing of
the body are so at all. We can sit up whole nights to game,
to dance, to revel, to see a mask or play; make nothing of
it. We can rise up early and go to bed late, for months
together, for our gain and profit, and be never the worse.
We can fast whole days together, and nor eat nor drink,
when we are eager upon our business or sport, and never
feel it. We can endure pain and cold and tendance,
affronts and injuries and neglects, slightings and re-
proaches too, to compass a little honour and preferment,
and not say a word. We can be temperate too, when we
please, for some ends and purposes. Only the soul's
business is not worth the while; whether "castaways" or
no, is not considerable; all is too much, on that account:
mole-hills are mountains, and there is a lion always in
the way—watching will kill us, fasting will destroy us,
any kind of strictness will impair us; temperance itself
will pine us into skeletons; every good exercise takes up
too much time; every petty thing that crosses but the
way is an unconquerable difficulty, a lion—when the
soul's business is to be gone about. . . .

But suppose thou art infirm indeed, and canst not do
so much as perhaps thou wouldst do else, canst thou do

nothing? If thou canst not watch, canst thou not fast sometimes? If thou canst not fast, canst thou not endure a little hunger, thirst, or cold, or pains, for Heaven, neither? If all these seem hard, canst thou not be temperate, neither? canst thou not bring thyself to it by degrees, by exercise, and practice, neither? Or if thou canst not watch a night, canst thou not watch an hour—do somewhat towards it? If thou canst not fast from all kind of meat, canst thou not abstain at least from some—from dainties and delicates? If not often, canst thou not at such a time as this, when all Christians ever used to do it? Sure, he that cannot fast a meal, may yet feed upon coarser fare. He that cannot do any of these long, may do all of them some time; may exercise himself in a little time to the hardest of them all. Let us, then, however, set a-doing somewhat; for God's sake let us ... do somewhat that is akin to the ancient piety.

39. THE ABIDING EASTER JOY

This [Easter Day] is a day when perplexities cannot stay, fears cannot tarry with us, our heads cannot long hang down; the news of it is so full of gladness, of comfort, and of joy. At the rising of this day's sun of righteousness, our perplexities pass away as the clouds before the sun; our tears melt as the dew before it; and we turn up our heads like flowers to the sunbeams. It is a day the fullest of all good tidings—as the seal and assurance of all the good news we heard before it. The angels fly everywhere about to-day, even into the grave, with comfortable messages. "Why weepest thou?" says one; "Fear not", says another; "Why seek" you "among the dead?" says a third. What do you at the grave?—"He is risen", says the whole choir; he whose rising is all your risings, who is your Saviour now complete, and the lifter up of all your heads; and go but into Galilee and you shall see him.

But this only hearing of him must for this time content us; we shall one day see him as he is; till then, if we hear of him with our ears, and feel him in our hearts, and see him in our conceits; if so hear him as to believe him risen, and our hearts listen to it. . . . if they do, we need not be the least perplexed for not visibly seeing him. All believers that then were did not see him so; five hundred, indeed, we read of, all at once; but they were not all that were then believers: "Not to all", says St Peter, expressly, "but unto witnesses chosen before of God." There is a blessedness, and it seems, by the manner of speaking, somewhat greater, for them "that have not seen, and yet have believed".

Be we then content to-day to hear that he "is risen", with the first news and tidings of it. From a good mouth it comes, to good souls it comes, in good time it comes; from the mouths of angels to good women, and very seasonably, when they were "much perplexed", much "afraid", and much cast down for want of such a message. And though we cannot here see Christ as we desire, yet be we pleased to see ourselves, our own sad condition upon the loss of him, in these women's perplexities, fears, and downcast looks—our way to seek him, humbly, with our faces down as not worthy to look up—reverently, with fear and trembling, as afraid to miss him—solicit-ously, much perplexed, to want him, as they were, in the text.

And that we may not give up our hope, be afraid, or cast down for ever, look we upon the bright "shining garments" of the two angels here (for these "men" are no less)—it is a joyful sight—and rejoice at the good success that always follows them that so seek him—angels and good news. The women found it here—heard the good news from the angels' lips. You must be content to hear it from mine; yet you know who says it, *Angelus Domini exercituum est*; "The priest is the angel" or messenger—that is enough—"of the Lord of hosts"; too much for me, poor sinful wretch. But look not upon me, but upon them that first told the news. . . .

The sum of all is this—That though it sometimes fall

out to us that we lose Christ, or cannot find him for a while, and so fall into perplexities and fears, and go up and down dejected, with downcast looks; yet if we so seek him with a solicitous love, a reverent fear, and humble diligence, we shall meet angels after a while, to comfort us and bring us news of our beloved Lord, and find him risen or rising in us ere we are aware.

And the close of all will be our duty, and the duty of the day, (1) to make ourselves sensible of the perplexed and sad estate of those that are without Christ, who have lost him in the grave, or know not where he is, or how to find him; and thereupon, (2) so set ourselves to seek him that we may be sure at last to hear of him, and be made partakers of his resurrection.

Ps. 24. 3, 4: "Who shall ascend into the hill of the Lord?
Or who shall stand up in his holy place? Even he that
hath clean hands, and a pure heart; and hath not lifted
up his soul unto vanity, nor sworn deceitfully to his
neighbour."

The Psalm is one of them which the Church appoints for
Ascension Day, and I see not but it may very well pass
for a kind of prophecy by way of an ecstatical admiration
at the sight of Christ's ascension. So it passed with the
Fathers, and with our fathers too,—may so with us; for
never was it so fulfilled to a tittle as by Christ and his
ascension. He, the only "he" of clean hands, and pure
heart, and holy mouth, and holy "all"; he the first that
entered Heaven, that got up the hill, that entered into
the "holy place not made with hands". Not any doors so
properly "everlasting" as those of Heaven, nor they ever
opened for "any king of glory to come in", as it is verse 7,
but him. I cannot tell how we should expound it otherwise, without much more metaphor and figure.

Yet I will allow it too for the prophet's admiration at
the foresight of the happiness of God's peculiar people,
and their condition: that God, whose "the whole earth
is and all its fullness", should out of all its places choose
Sion for his place; he "whose the world is, and all that
dwell therein", as it follows there, should choose out the
Jews, amongst all the dwellers, to dwell among, them

only to serve him upon that hill; that, further, this God, whose all is, should still of this "all" so particularly honour some as to give them the privilege of his hill and holy place, his solemn worship and service, to go up first into his holy places upon earth, and then afterwards ascend into the "holy places"—the Heavens—for the word means one as well as the other. Who are they? What a sort of people are they that are so happy, so much exalted upon the earth, and over it! It is worth the admiring, worth the inquiring, and we find it presently who they be, even such as have "clean hands", and "pure hearts", that "lift not up their minds to vanity, nor their mouths to wickedness or deceit".

In sum, these are the only men that shall ascend those everlasting hills, those eternal holy places, that are only worthy to enter into God's houses and holy places of the earth too, obtain those admirable privileges that are innocent and pure, and just and true, the only men worth the admiring, as the Church and Heaven, the hill of the Lord and his holy place, are the only things are worth it; Heaven is for none but such, and when we enter into the holy places we should all be such, as none have right to enter them indeed but such.

The wind blows where it lists, on this side or on that side, or on any side, anywhere, and everywhere. The Spirit does so too, only with more propriety to *ubi vult*, doing out of the liberty of its own will, what the wind only does out of the subtilty of its nature. No place lies exempted from the power of his will. It finds St Paul and Silas in the prison, and blows up the organs of their voices into songs and hymns. It finds Manasseh in the dungeon, blows there with his wind, and the waters flow out of his eyes. It finds St Matthew at the receipt of custom, and blows him out of a publican into an apostle. It blows St Peter and St Andrew out of their boat to the stern of the Church of Christ. He blows upon some in their journey, as upon St Paul; upon others at home, as upon Cornelius; upon one in the bed, upon another at the mill, upon Jonas in the whale's belly. No place beyond his compass, not the isles of the Gentiles, not the land of Uz, not the deserts of Arabia. Here and there, even amongst them, he blows some into his kingdom. In a word, no chamber so secret, but it can get into; no place so remote, but it can reach; none so private, but it can find; none so strong, but it can break through; none so deep, but it can fathom; none so high, but it can scale; no place at all, but it can come into; and none so bad, but some way or other it will vouchsafe to visit.

It makes holy David cry out as in an ecstasy, "Whither shall I go then from thy Spirit? or whither shall I go then from thy presence? If I climb up into heaven, thou art there; if I go down to hell, thou art there also. If I take the wings of the morning, and remain in the uttermost parts of the earth, even there also shall thy hand lead me, and thy right hand shall hold me." No place, it seems, in heaven, or earth, or sea, or hell itself, can hold him out.

Nor can any hold him to this or that way of working, neither; for he bloweth how he lists; sometimes louder, sometimes softer, sometimes after this manner, sometimes after that. He raises new inclinations, or he cherishes the old; he changes the tempers of men or disposes them; he removes opportunities of doing ill, or he propounds opportunities of doing good; he scares us with threats or allures us with promises; he drives us with judgements, or he draws us with mercies; he inflames us within, or he moves us from without, which way soever it pleases him.

No wind so various in its blowing. Different ways he has to deal with divers men: and "diversities of gifts" he has for them too, "differences of administrations, diversities of operations". To one he gives the "word of wisdom", to another the "word of knowledge", to another "faith", to another the "gift of healing", to another the "working of miracles", to another "prophecy", to another "discerning of spirits", to another "divers kinds of tongues", to another the "interpretation of tongues", all from the Spirit, says the Apostle, in the forecited chapter.

Nor was this only for those times. He still breathes diversities of gifts and graces, as he pleases. On some, sanctifying graces; on others, edifying, on others both. To some he gives a cheerful, to others a sad spirit; to some a kind of holy lightness; to others a religious gravity; to one a power wholly to quit the world; to another, power to stand holy in it; to one, an ability to rule, to another a readiness to obey; to one courage, to another patience, to a third temperance, and so to others other graces, as he thinks fittest.

42. PREPARATION FOR HOLY COMMUNION

The Lord is at hand in the blessed sacrament; and that is also now at hand, but a week between us and it. And moderation of all kinds is but a due preparation to it, some special act of it to be done against it. "Righteousness and equity is the habitation of his seat", says David; the Lord sits not nor abides where they are not. The holy sacrament that is his seat, a seat of wonder, is not set but in the righteous and good soul, has no efficacy but there. Modesty and humility are the steps to it; into the modest and humble soul only will he vouchsafe to come. All reverence and civility is but requisite in our addresses unto it.

But moderation, meekness, and patience, and sweetness, and forgiving injuries is so requisite, that there is no coming there, no offering at the altar, till we be first reconciled to our brother. "Go, be first reconciled to thy brother", says our Lord himself; so that now if we desire a blessing of the blessed sacrament unto us, if we desire the Lord should there come to us, "let our moderation be known to all men" before we come.

Let us study the art of reconcilement; let us not stand upon points of honour or punctilios with our brother, upon quirks and niceties; let us part with somewhat of our right; let us do it civilly, use all men with courtesy and civility, express all modesty and sweetness in our conversation; all softness and moderation, patience and meekness, gentleness and loving-kindness towards all, even the bitterest of our enemies; considering "the Lord is at hand": the Lord of righteousness expects our righteousness and equity; the Lord in his body, and looks for the reverent and handsome behaviour of our bodies; the Lord of pure eyes, and cannot endure any unseemliness or intemperance either in our inward or outward man; the Lord that died and suffered for us, and upon that score requires we should be content to suffer also anything for him, not to be angry, or troubled, or repine, or murmur at it, or at them that cause it. At the holy sacrament he is so near at hand, that he is at the table with us; reaches to every one a portion of himself, yet will give it to none but such as come in an universal charity, with all the forementioned moderations.

43. GOD'S PLEASURE IN HIS SAINTS

Ps. 149: "Such honour have all his saints."

So the text, so the day [All Saints' Day]—a day dedicated to God in honour of "all his saints". "Such honour" has God allowed them, "such honour" has the holy Church bestowed upon them. Because they are "his", and as his here they are had in honour; because his holy ones, *sancti ejus*, as his saints, or holy ones, honoured with a holy day; or, if you will, God honoured in them on the day. For this honour also have all the saints, that all the honour done to them, all the honour done by them, by the saints in earth to the saints in Heaven, all the virtues of the one, all the praises of the other, are to the honour, and praise, and glory of God, in all the "congregations of the saints", whether in Heaven or earth.

It is not fit, therefore, any of them should be forgotten, from whose memories God receives so much; not reasonable to refuse them any honour that so redounds to God's. The Psalm gives them it, and the day gives them it; God says they shall have this honour, and the Church this day pays it, and we must pay it, if we honour either him or her, God or the Church, or father or mother; pay it to them all—to all to whom it is due, all honour that is due. This is a day for us to meet all together to pay it in, for them all together to receive it in. We cannot do it to all severally, they are too many, we may do it to all together. We profess a great article of our faith, the Communion of Saints, by doing it. . . .

And greater yet; for it is not *honor* but *gloria* here— *et sancti in gloria*— a glorious honour that the saints are honoured with. . . . honour, joy, and glory given to them "in their beds", to have joy and honour conferred upon them "in their beds", to have it, as it were, with ease, with lying still, and to enjoy it with security, without fear of rousing from it, and in the very beds of dust, the dark chambers of the grave, the mansions of death itself, to have this light and glory shine upon them, to have security and peace, ease and pleasure established on their glory, and those melancholy rooms that are hanged with worms and rottenness enlightened with the beams of perpetual joy and comfort, is a vast addition to their glory. Yet this they have, not only an immarcescible and incorruptible "crown of glory", laid up for them, but their very "bones flourish out of the grave"; and even the lodgings of their very ashes seem to exult with a kind of joy to be made the receptacles and cabinets of those jewels of the Almighty, and their sepulchres and memorials are blessed for evermore. The very places where they come are joyful at their shadows as they pass by; miracles have been done by their shadows whilst they passed by; and when their bones have lain awhile silent in the grave, the dead have yet been raised by them to life again.

44. THE PRIESTHOOD PREPARES THE WAY FOR CHRIST'S COMING

Mark 1. 3: "Prepare ye the way of the Lord, make his paths straight."

The ministers and preachers of the Word are the public messengers and harbingers who are sent to prepare the Lord's way (as St John Baptist was) before him: yet every one must sweep his own door. For the words are by St John Baptist preached to all Pharisees and Sadducees, publicans, and soldiers, and all the people that came to him; every one to have a share: and so he gives it them; tells people, and publicans, and soldiers what to do; sets every one his path, his part of the way to prepare and straighten. Give me leave to do so too.

The ministers of the Gospel, they come first; they have the greatest share with St John Baptist, to go before the face of the Lord to prepare his way. But how? 1. "To give knowledge of salvation", says old Zachary, "to his people, for the remission of sins"; or somewhat more, even to give remission too, to give absolution; so to give knowledge to the people, or instruct them, and to absolve them, is some part at least of the minister's share; but to baptize also with the Baptist, and to consecrate with Christ himself, is to prepare his way too, to make way for him. To raise the valleys; to comfort the dejected, the cast down and afflicted soul against his sorrows, the penitent against his sins, the fearful against the fear of death, the weak-hearted against trouble and persecution; to encourage them to lift up their heads and look to the recompense of reward, to raise up the grovelling souls of men from earth and flesh to heaven and heavenly business. 2. To cast down the mountains of pride and singularity, schism and heresy, that lift up themselves against the obedience of Christ. 3. To rectify the perverse and crooked souls of men. And 4. To smooth and soften them: to lay the way of Christ smooth and plain before them, make them know his yoke is easy and his burthen light, by continual preaching to them, and instructing them, so preparing them for the way of Christ.

Thus the minister prepares his way in the people's hearts; sometimes cleansing the young infant's way by baptism, and sometimes rectifying the young and old man's ways by advice and exhortation; sometimes clearing them with absolution, sometimes purifying them with the holy Sacrament, some way or other always preparing them against the Lord's coming. And it lies upon him so to do.

JEREMY TAYLOR (1613–67)

Jeremy Taylor's life, in its vicissitudes of honours and misfortunes, was highly characteristic of almost any prominent man in the seventeenth century. Gifted with brilliant powers of intellect and speech, he early in life won Laud's favour and promotion to the living of Uppingham and a royal chaplaincy.

But troubles followed as the sparks fly upward. Captured as a royal chaplain after a battle near Cardigan Castle, he was released through the offices of the Earl of Carbery, and became chaplain to that peer's household at Golden Grove.

In this Welsh retreat he wrote his most famous sermons, the *Liberty of Prophesying*, and other famous books. Occasionally, at considerable risk to himself, he visited his London publisher, and even preached at the one church which Cromwell permitted to function in London, St Gregory's, near St Paul's.

At times in great poverty, he twice in this period suffered short terms of imprisonment, the second time in Chepstow Castle on his return journey to Golden Grove. When released, he was given shelter by a Welsh lady who later married him.

In 1657 he ran great risks to minister for some months privately in the houses of Anglican friends in London, who (one was John Evelyn) supported him in return for his ministrations as celebrant or confessor.

In 1658 he became private chaplain to Lord Conway, in Ireland, where he made cultured and kindly friends. But his position, under the Commonwealth, was illegal, and local Presbyterian ministers persecuted him with charges of "Popery". Once more he suffered a short imprisonment.

In 1660 he managed to get to London, and join in the enthusiastic reception of Charles II. Three months later, he was appointed to the Irish See of Down and Connor—not only for his long loyalty to the Crown, but also because he was by now the greatest living English theologian.

In Ireland, however, the clergy of his diocese were bitter Presbyterians who refused to attend his synods and even threatened his life. His chief comfort was his appointment as Vice-Chancellor to Dublin University, where he worked a great reformation in education and learning. In spite of his views on religious toleration, he felt bound to seek the help of the secular arm to expel his Presbyterian clergy, and filled their parishes with priests from England. To the end of his days he longed for a more congenial sphere, but none was given him.

His sermons, enriched by abundant illustrations, great learning, and glowing imagery, had made him the most famous preacher of the day, and he won great respect by his holy character.

45. THE LOVE OF WIFE AND CHILDREN

When a man dwells in love, then the breasts of his wife are pleasant as the droppings upon the hill of Hermon, her eyes are fair as the light of heaven, she is a fountain sealed, and he can quench his thirst, and ease his cares, and lay his sorrows down upon her lap, and can retire home to his sanctuary and refectory, and his gardens of sweetness and chaste refreshments. No man can tell but he that loves his children, how many delicious accents make a man's heart dance in the pretty conversation of those dear pledges; their childishness, their stammering, their little angers, their innocence, their imperfections, their necessities are so many little emanations of joy and comfort to him that delights in their persons and society; but he that loves not his wife and children, feeds a lioness at home, and broods a nest of sorrows; and blessing itself cannot make him happy; so that all the commandments of God enjoining a man to "love his wife", are nothing but so many necessities and capacities of joy. "She that is loved is safe, and he that loves is joyful."

Love is a union of all things excellent; it contains in it proportion, and satisfaction, and rest, and confidence; and I wish that this were so much proceeded in, that the heathens themselves could not go beyond us in this virtue, and its proper, and its appendant happiness. Tiberius Gracchus chose to die for the safety of his wife; and yet methinks to a Christian to do so, should be no hard thing; for many servants will die for their masters, and many gentlemen will die for their friend; but the examples are not so many of those that are ready to do it for their dearest relatives, and yet some there have been. Baptista Fregosa tells of a Neapolitan that gave himself a slave to the Moors, that he might follow his wife; and Dominicus Catalusius, the prince of Lesbos, kept company with his lady when she was a leper; and these are greater things than to die.

46. HOLY MARRIAGE AND CELIBACY

Marriage was ordained by God, instituted in Paradise, was the relief of a natural necessity, and the first blessing from the Lord; he gave to man not a friend, but a wife, that is, a friend and a wife too (for a good woman is in her soul the same that a man is, and she is a woman only in her body; that she may have the excellency of the one, and the usefulness of the other, and become amiable in both). It is the seminary of the Church, and daily brings forth sons and daughters unto God; it was ministered to by angels, and Raphael waited upon a young man that he might have a blessed marriage, and that that marriage might repair two sad families, and bless all their relatives. Our blessed Lord, though he was born of a maiden, yet she was veiled under the cover of marriage, and she was married to a widower; for Joseph the supposed father of our Lord had children by a former wife. The first miracle that ever Jesus did, was to do honour to a wedding; marriage was in the world before sin, and is in all ages of the world the greatest and most effective antidote against sin, in which all the world had perished if God had not made a remedy; and although sin hath soured marriage, and stuck the man's head with cares, and the woman's bed with sorrows in the production of children, yet these are but throes of life and glory; and "she shall be saved in childbearing, if she be found in faith and righteousness".

Marriage is a school and exercise of virtue; and though

marriage hath cares, yet the single life hath desires which are more troublesome and more dangerous, and often end in sin, while the cares are but instances of duty and exercises of piety; and therefore if single life hath more privacy of devotion, yet marriage hath more necessities and more variety of it, and is an exercise of more graces. In two virtues, celibacy or single life may have the advantages of degrees ordinarily and commonly—that is, in chastity and devotion: but as in some persons this may fail, and it does in very many, and a married man may spend as much time in devotion as any virgins or widows do, yet as in marriage even those virtues of chastity and devotion are exercised: so in other instances, this state hath proper exercises and trials for those graces, for which single life can never be crowned. Here is the proper scene of piety and patience, of the duty of parents and the charity of relatives; here kindness is spread abroad, and love is united and made firm as a centre: marriage is the nursery of Heaven; the virgin sends prayers to God, but she carries but one soul to him; but the state of marriage fills up the numbers of the elect, and hath in it the labour of love, and the delicacies of friendship, the blessing of society, and the union of hands and hearts; it hath in it less of beauty, but more of safety than the single life; it hath more care, but less danger; it is more merry, and more sad; is fuller of sorrows, and fuller of joys; it lies under more burdens, but is supported by all the strengths of love and charity, and those burdens are delightful.

Marriage is the mother of the world, and preserves

kingdoms, and fills cities, and churches, and Heaven itself. Celibate, like the fly in the heart of an apple, dwells in a perpetual sweetness, but sits alone and is confined and dies in singularity; but marriage, like the useful bee, builds a house, and gathers sweetness from every flower, and labours and unites into societies and republics, and sends out colonies, and feeds the world with delicacies, and obeys their king, and keeps order, and exercises many virtues, and promotes the interest of mankind, and is that state of good things to which God hath designed the present constitution of the world. . . . Single life makes men in one instance to be like angels, but marriage in very many things makes the chaste pair to be like to Christ. "This is a great mystery", but it is the symbolical and sacramental representation of the greatest mysteries of our religion. Christ descended from his Father's bosom, and contracted his divinity with flesh and blood, and married our nature, and we became a Church, the spouse of the Bridegroom, which he cleansed with his blood, and gave her his Holy Spirit for a dowry, and Heaven for a jointure; begetting children unto God by the gospel. This spouse he hath joined to himself by an excellent charity, he feeds her at his own table, and lodges her nigh his own heart, provides for all her necessities, relieves her sorrows, determines her doubts, guides her wanderings, he is become her head, and she as a signet upon his right hand; he first indeed was betrothed to the Synagogue, and had many children by her, but she forsook her love, and then he married the Church of the Gentiles, and by her as by a second venter had a more numerous issue, *atque una domus est omnium filiorum ejus*, all the children dwell in the same house, and are heirs of the same promises, entitled to the same inheritance.

47. SELF-JUDGEMENT AS PREPARATION FOR THE LAST JUDGEMENT

Cannot the accuser[1] truly say to the Judge concerning such persons, "They were thine by creation, but mine by their own choice; thou didst redeem them indeed, but they sold themselves to me for a trifle, or for an unsatisfying interest: thou diedst for them, but they obeyed my commandments: I gave them nothing, I promised them nothing but the filthy pleasure of a night, or the joys of madness, or the delights of a disease: I never hanged upon the cross three long hours for them, nor endured the labours of a poor life thirty-three years together for their interest: only when they were thine by the merit of thy death, they quickly became mine by the demerit of their ingratitude; and when thou hadst clothed their soul with thy robe, and adorned them by thy graces, we stripped them naked as their shame, and only put on a robe of darkness, and they thought themselves secure and went dancing to their grave, like a drunkard to a fight, or a fly unto a candle; and therefore, they that did partake with us in our faults, must divide with us in our portion and fearful interest"?

This is a sad story, because it ends in death, and there is nothing to abate or lessen the calamity. It concerns us, therefore, to consider in time, that he that tempts us will accuse us, and what he calls pleasant now, he shall then say was nothing, and all the gains that now invite earthly

[1] I.e., διάβολος, the devil.

souls and mean persons to vanity, were nothing but the seeds of folly, and the harvest is pain, and sorrow, and shame eternal.

But then, since this horror proceeds upon the account of so many accusers, God hath put it into our power, by a timely accusation of ourselves in the tribunal of the court Christian, to prevent all the arts of aggravation, which at domesday shall load foolish and undiscerning souls.

He that accuses himself of his crimes here, means to forsake them, and looks upon them on all sides, and spies out his deformity, and is taught to hate them, he is instructed and prayed for, he prevents the anger of God, and defeats the devil's malice; and, by making shame the instrument of repentance, he takes away the sting, and makes that to be his medicine, which otherwise would be his death. And concerning this exercise, I shall only add what the patriarch of Alexandria told an old religious person in his hermitage. Having asked him what he found in that desert, he was answered only thus, "*Indesinenter culpare et judicare meipsum*; To judge and condemn myself perpetually, that is the employment of my solitude." The patriarch answered, "*Non est alia via*; There is no other way."

By accusing ourselves we shall make the devil's malice useless, and our own consciences clear, and be reconciled to the Judge by the severities of an early repentance, and then we need to fear no accusers.

48. A PEACEFUL HEART A NECESSITY
FOR TRUE PRAYER

Anger . . . is a fever in the heart, and a calenture in the head, and a fire in the face, and a sword in the hand, and a fury all over; and therefore can never suffer a man to be in a disposition to pray. For prayer is an action, and a state of intercourse and desire, exactly contrary to this character of anger.

Prayer is an action of likeness to the Holy Ghost, the Spirit of gentleness and dove-like simplicity; an imitation of the holy Jesus, whose spirit is meek, up to the greatness of the biggest example, and a conformity to God; whose anger is always just, and marches slowly, and is without transportation, and often hindered, and never hasty, and is full of mercy: prayer is the peace of our spirit, the stillness of our thoughts, the evenness of recollection, the seat of meditation, the rest of our cares, and the calm of our tempest; prayer is the issue of a quiet mind, of untroubled thoughts, it is the daughter of charity, and the sister of meekness; and he that prays to God with an angry, that is, with a troubled and discomposed spirit, is like him that retires into a barrel to meditate, and sets up his closet in the out-quarters of an army, and chooses a frontier-garrison to be wise in.

Anger is a perfect alienation of the mind from prayer, and therefore is contrary to that attention, which presents our prayers in a right line to God. For so have I seen a lark rising from his bed of grass, and soaring upwards, singing as he rises, and hopes to get to heaven, and climb above the clouds; but the poor bird was beaten back with the loud sighings of an eastern wind, and his motion made irregular and inconstant, descending more at every breath of the tempest, than it could recover by the libration and frequent weighing of his wings; till the little creature was forced to sit down and pant, and stay till the storm was over, and then it made a prosperous flight, and did rise and sing, as if it had learned music and motion from an angel as he passed sometimes through the air, about his ministries here below. So is the prayer of a good man; when his affairs have required business, and his business was matter of discipline, and his discipline was to pass upon a sinning person, or had a design of charity, his duty met with infirmities of a man, and anger was its instrument, and the instrument became stronger than the prime agent, and raised a tempest, and overruled the man; and then his prayer was broken, and his thoughts were troubled, and his words went up towards a cloud, and his thoughts pulled them back again, and made them without intention; and the good man sighs for his infirmity, but must be content to lose the prayer, and he must recover it when his anger is removed, and his spirit is becalmed, made even as the brow of Jesus, and smooth like the heart of God; and then it ascends to Heaven upon the wings of the holy dove, and dwells with God, till it returns, like the useful bee, loaden with a blessing and the dew of Heaven.

49. CHRIST'S SUFFERINGS

He entered into the world with all the circumstances of poverty. He had a star to illustrate his birth; but a stable for his bedchamber, and a manger for his cradle. The angels sang hymns when he was born; but he was cold and cried, uneasy and unprovided. He lived long in the trade of a carpenter; he, by whom God made the world, had, in his first years, the business of a mean and ignoble trade. He did good wherever he went; and almost wherever he went, was abused. He deserved Heaven for his obedience, but found a cross in his way thither: and if ever any man had reason to expect fair usages from God, and to be dandled in the lap of ease, softness, and a prosperous fortune, he it was only that could deserve that, or any thing that can be good. But, after he had chosen to live a life of virtue, of poverty, and labour, he entered into a state of death; whose shame and trouble were great enough to pay for the sins of the whole world.

And I shall choose to express this mystery in the words of Scripture. He died not by a single or a sudden death, but he was the "Lamb slain from the beginning of the world": for he was massacred in Abel, saith St Paulinus; he was tossed upon the waves of the sea in the person of Noah; it was he that went out of his country, when Abraham was called from Charran, and wandered from his native soil; he was offered up in Isaac, persecuted in Jacob, betrayed in Joseph, blinded in Samson, affronted in Moses, sawed in Isaiah, cast into the dungeon with

Jeremiah: for all these were types of Christ suffering. And then his passion continued even after his resurrection. For it is he that suffers in all his members; it is he that "endures the contradiction of all sinners"; it is he that is "the Lord of life, and is crucified again, and put to open shame" in all the sufferings of his servants, and sins of rebels, and defiances of apostates and renegadoes, and violence of tyrants, and injustice of usurpers, and the persecutions of his Church. It is he that is stoned in St Stephen, flayed in the person of St Bartholomew: he was roasted upon St Laurence's gridiron, exposed to lions in St Ignatius, burnt in St Polycarp, frozen in the lake where stood forty martyrs of Cappadocia. *"Unigenitus enim Dei ad peragendum mortis suae sacramentum consummavit omne genus humanarum passionum"*, said St Hilary; "The sacrament of Christ's death is not to be accomplished but by suffering all the sorrows of humanity."

All that Christ came for, was, or was mingled with, sufferings: for all those little joys which God sent, either to recreate his person, or to illustrate his office, were abated, or attended with afflictions; God being more careful to establish in him the covenant of sufferings, than to refresh his sorrows. Presently after the angels had finished their hallelujahs, he was forced to fly to save his life; and the air became full of shrieks of the desolate mothers of Bethlehem for their dying babes. God had no sooner made him illustrious with a voice from Heaven, and the descent of the Holy Ghost upon him in the waters of baptism, but he was delivered over to be tempted and assaulted by the devil in the wilderness. His transfiguration was a bright ray of glory; but then also he entered into a cloud, and was told a sad story what he was to suffer at Jerusalem. And upon Palm Sunday, when he rode triumphantly into Jerusalem, and was adorned with the acclamations of a King and a God, he wet the palms with his tears, sweeter than the drops of manna, or the little pearls of Heaven, that descended upon Mount Hermon; weeping, in the midst of this triumph, over obstinate, perishing, and malicious Jerusalem.

For this Jesus was like the rainbow, which God set in the clouds as a sacrament to confirm a promise, and establish a grace; he was half made of the glories of the light, and half of the moisture of a cloud; in his best days he was but half triumph and half sorrow: he was sent to tell of his Father's mercies, and that God intended to spare us; but appeared not but in the company or in the retinue of a shower, and of foul weather.

But I need not tell that Jesus, beloved of God, was a suffering person: that which concerns this question most, is, that he made for us a covenant of sufferings: his doctrines were such as expressly and by consequent enjoin and suppose sufferings, and a state of affliction; his very promises were sufferings; his beatitudes were sufferings; his rewards, and his arguments to invite men to follow him, were only taken from sufferings in this life, and the reward of sufferings hereafter.

50. THE POWER OF PRAYER

I sum up all in the words of God by the prophet; "Run to and fro through the streets of Jerusalem, and see, and know, and seek in the broad places thereof, if you can find a man; if there be any that executeth judgement, that seeketh truth", *"virum quaerentem fidem"*, "a man that seeketh for faith"; *"et propitius ero ei"*, "and I will pardon it". God would pardon all Jerusalem for one good man's sake; there are such days and opportunities of mercy, when God, at the prayer of one holy person, will save a people; and Ruffinus spake a great thing, but it was hugely true; *"Quis dubitet mundum stare precibus sanctorum?"* "the world itself is established and kept from dissolution by the prayers of saints"; and the prayers of saints shall hasten the day of judgement; and we cannot easily find two effects greater. But there are many other very great ones; for the prayers of holy men appease God's wrath, drive away temptations, and resist and overcome the devil: holy prayer procures the ministry and service of angels, it rescinds the decrees of God, it cures sicknesses and obtains pardon, it arrests the sun in its course, and stays the wheels of the chariot of the moon; it rules over all God's creatures, and opens and shuts the storehouses of rain; it unlocks the cabinet of the womb, and quenches the violence of fire; it stops the mouths of lions, and reconciles our sufferance and weak faculties, with the violence of torment and sharpness of persecution; it pleases God and supplies all our needs.

But prayer that can do thus much for us, can do nothing at all without holiness; for "God heareth not sinners, but if any man be a worshipper of God, and doth his will, him he heareth."

51. TRUE PRAYER LEADS TO INTERCESSION

God hath appointed some persons and callings of men to pray for others; such are fathers for their children, bishops for their dioceses, kings for their subjects, and the whole order ecclesiastical for all the men and women in the Christian Church. And it is well it is so; for, as things are now and have been too long, how few are there that understand it to be their duty, or part of their necessary employment, that some of their time, and much of their prayers, and an equal portion of their desires, be spent upon the necessities of others. All men do not think it necessary, and fewer practise it frequently, and they but coldly, without interest and deep resentment: it is like the compassion we have in other men's miseries, we are not concerned in it, and it is not our ease, and our hearts ache not when another man's children are made fatherless, or his wife a sad widow: and just so are our prayers for their relief. If we thought their evils to be ours—if we and they, as members of the same body, had sensible and real communications of good and evil—if we understood what is really meant by being "members one of another", or if we did not think it a spiritual word of art, instrumental only to a science, but no part of duty or real relation—surely we should pray more earnestly one for another than we usually do.[1]

[1] When we remember that these sermons were published in 1651, only two years after the King's execution, and when bishops

How few of us are troubled, when he sees his brother wicked or dishonourably vicious? Who is sad and melancholy when his neighbour is almost in hell? when he sees him grow old in iniquity? How many days have we set apart for the public relief and interests of the kingdom? How earnestly have we fasted, if our prince be sick or afflicted? What alms have we given for our brother's conversion? Or if this be great, how importunate and passionate have we been with God by prayer in his behalf, by prayer and secret petition?

But, however, though it were well, very well, that all of us would think of this duty a little more; because, besides the excellency of the duty itself, it would have this blessed consequent, that for whose necessities we pray, if we do desire earnestly they should be relieved, we would, whenever we can and in all we can, set our hands to it; and if we pity the orphan-children and pray for them heartily, we would also, when we could, relieve them charitably: but though it were therefore very well that things were thus with all men, yet God, who takes care of us all, makes provision for us in special manner; and the whole order of the clergy are appointed by God to pray for others, to be ministers of Christ's priesthood, to be followers of his advocation, to stand between God and his people, and to present before God all their needs and all their desires.

were forbidden to ordain and the use of the Prayer Book had been prohibited already for six years, and many of the clergy were in dire distress and poverty, we can realize how intercession might hold great place in the minds of Taylor's hearers. G. L. M.

52. THE MIRACLES OF THE DIVINE MERCY

Man, having destroyed that which God delighted in, that is, the beauty of his soul, fell into an evil portion, and being seized upon by the divine justice, grew miserable, and condemned to an incurable sorrow. Poor Adam, being banished and undone, went and lived a sad life in the mountains of India, and turned his face and his prayers towards Paradise; thither he sent his sighs, to that place he directed his devotions, there was his heart now, where his felicity sometimes had been: but he knew not how to return thither, for God was his enemy, and, by many of his attributes, opposed himself against him. God's power was armed against him; and poor man, whom a fly or a fish could kill, was assaulted and beaten with a sword of fire in the hand of a cherubim. God's eye watched him, his omniscience was man's accuser, his severity was the judge, his justice the executioner. It was a mighty calamity that man was to undergo, when he that made him armed himself against his creature, which would have died or turned to nothing, if he had but withdrawn the miracles and the almightiness of his power: if God had taken his arm from under him, man had perished.

But it was, therefore, a greater evil when God laid his arm upon him and against him, and seemed to support him, that he might be longer killing him.

In the midst of these sadnesses God remembered his

own creature, and pitied it; and, by his mercy, rescued him from the hands of his power, and the sword of his justice, and the guilt of his punishment, and the disorder of his sin; and placed him in that order of good things where he ought to have stood.

It was mercy that preserved the noblest of God's creatures here below; he who stood condemned and undone under all the other attributes of God, was only saved and rescued by his mercy; that it may be evident that God's mercy is above all his works, and above all ours, greater than the creation, and greater than our sins. As is his majesty, so is his mercy, that is, without measures and without rules, sitting in Heaven and filling all the world, calling for a duty that he may give a blessing, making man that he may save him, punishing him that he may preserve him. And God's justice bowed down to his mercy, and all his power passed into mercy, and his omniscience converted into care and watchfulness, into providence and observation for man's avail; and Heaven gave its influence for man, and rained showers for our food and drink; and the attributes and acts of God sat at the foot of mercy, and all that mercy descended upon the head of man. For so the light of the world in the morning of the creation was spread abroad like a curtain, and dwelt no where, but filled the *expansum* with a dissemination great as the unfoldings of the air's looser garment, or the wilder fringes of the fire . . . and all the light of the world became the body of the sun; and he lent some to his weaker sister that walks in the night, and guides a traveller, and teaches him to distinguish a house from a river, or a rock from a plain field. So is the mercy of God, a vast *expansum* and a huge ocean; from eternal ages it dwelt round about the throne of God, and it filled all that infinite distance and space, that hath no measures but the will of God: until God, desiring to communicate that excellency and make it relative, created angels, that he might have persons capable of huge gifts; and man, who he knew would need forgiveness.

For so the angels, our elder brothers, dwelt for ever in the house of their Father, and never brake his commandments; but we, the younger, like prodigals, forsook our Father's house, and went into a strange country, and followed stranger courses, and spent the portion of our nature, and forfeited all our title to the family, and came to need another portion.

For, ever since the fall of Adam—who, like an unfortunate man, spent all that a wretched man could need, or a happy man could have—our life is repentance, and forgiveness is all our portion; and though angels were objects of God's bounty, yet man only is, in proper speaking, the object of his mercy: and the mercy which dwelt in an infinite circle, became confined to a little ring, and dwelt here below; and here shall dwell below, till it hath carried all God's portion up to Heaven, where it shall reign in glory upon our crowned heads for ever and ever!

53. THE INGRATITUDE OF NON-REPENTANCE

The purpose of our embassy and ministry is a prosecution of the mercies of God, and the work of redemption, and the intercession and mediation of Christ: it is the work of atonement and reconciliation that God designed, and Christ died for, and still prays for, and we preach for, and you all must labour for.

And therefore here consider, if it be not infinite impiety to "despise the riches of such a goodness", which at so great a charge, with such infinite labour and deep mysterious arts, invites us to repentance; that is, to such a thing as could not be granted to us unless Christ should die to purchase it; such a glorious favour, that is the issue of Christ's prayers in Heaven, and of all his labours, his sorrows, and his sufferings on earth. . . .

After the enumeration of these glories, these prodigies of mercies and loving-kindnesses, of Christ's dying for us, and interceding for us, and merely that we may repent and be saved, I shall less need to instance those other particularities whereby God continues, as by so many arguments of kindness, to sweeten our natures, and make them malleable to the precepts of love and obedience, the twin daughters of holy repentance: but the poorest person amongst us, besides the blessings and graces already reckoned, hath enough about him, and the accidents of every day, to shame him into repentance.

Does not God send "His angels to keep thee in all thy

ways?" Are not they ministering spirits sent forth to wait upon thee as thy guard? Art not thou kept from drowning, from fracture of bones, from madness, from deformities, by the riches of the divine goodness? Tell the joints of thy body; dost thou want a finger? And if thou dost not understand how great a blessing that is, do but remember how ill thou canst spare the use of it when thou hast but a thorn in it. The very privative blessings, the blessings of immunity, safeguard, and integrity, which we all enjoy, deserve a thanksgiving of a whole life.

If God should send a cancer upon thy face, or a wolf into thy breast, if he should spread a crust of leprosy upon thy skin, what wouldest thou give to be but as now thou art? Wouldest thou not repent of thy sins upon that condition? Which is the greater blessing? To be kept from them, or to be cured of them? And why therefore shall not this greater blessing lead thee to repentance? Why do we, not so aptly, promise repentance when we are sick, upon the condition to be made well, and yet perpetually forget it when we are well? As if health never were a blessing but when we have it not. Rather I fear the reason is, that when we are sick we promise to repent, because then we cannot sin the sins of our former life; but in health our appetites return to their capacity, and in all the way "we despise the riches of the divine goodness" which preserves us from such evils, which would be full of horror and amazement, if they should happen to us.

Hath God made any of you all chapfallen? Are you

affrighted with spectres and illusions of the spirits of darkness? How many earthquakes have you been in? How many days have any of you wanted bread? How many nights have you been without sleep? Are any of you distracted of your senses? And if God gives you meat and drink, health and sleep, proper seasons of the year, entire senses and a useful understanding; what a great unworthiness is it to be unthankful to so good a God, so benign a Father, so gracious a Lord? All the evils and baseness of the world can show nothing baser and more unworthy than ingratitude: and therefore it was not unreasonably said of Aristotle, Εὐτυχία φιλόθεος, "Prosperity makes a man love God", supposing men to have so much humanity left in them, as to love him from whom they have received so many favours. . . . And if any man whom God hath used to no other method but of his sweetness and the effusion of mercies, brings no other fruits but the apples of Sodom in return of all his culture and labours, God will cut off that unprofitable branch, that with Sodom it may suffer the flames of ever-lasting burning.

54. TAYLOR, NOW AN IRISH BISHOP, INSTRUCTS HIS PURITAN-MINDED CLERGY HOW TO PREACH AND TEACH WISELY

Passages from his Sermon at his first Visitation

What good can come from that which fools begin, and wise men can never end but by silence? And that had been the best way at first, and would have stifled them in the cradle. What have your people to do whether Christ's body be in the sacrament by consubstantiation, or transubstantiation; whether purgatory be in the centre of the earth, or in the air, or any where, or no where; and who but a madman would trouble their heads with the entangled links of the fantastic chain of predestination?

Teach them to fear God and honour the king, to keep the commandments of God, and the king's commands, because of the oath of God; learn them to be sober and temperate, to be just and to pay their debts, to speak well of their neighbours and to think meanly of themselves; teach them charity, and learn them to be zealous of good works.

Is it not a shame that the people should be filled with sermons against ceremonies, and declamations against a surplice, and tedious harangues against the poor airy sign of the cross in baptism? These things teach them to be ignorant; it fills them with wind, and they suck dry nurses; it makes them lazy and useless, troublesome and good for nothing. Can the definition of a Christian be, that a Christian is a man that rails against bishops and the common prayer-book? And yet this is the great labour of our neighbours that are crept in among us;[1] this they call the work of the Lord, and this is the great matter of the desired reformation; in these things they spend their long breath, and about these things they spend earnest prayers, and by these they judge their brother, and for these they revile their superior, and in this doughty cause they think it fit to fight and die.

Dress your people unto the imagery of Christ, dress them for their funerals, help them to make their accounts up, against the day of judgement.

I have known some persons and some families that would religiously educate their children, and bring them up in the Scriptures from their cradle; and they would teach them to tell who was the first man, and who was the oldest, and who was the wisest, and who was the strongest; but I never observed them to ask who was the best, and what things were required to make a man good; the Apostles' Creed was not the entertainment of their pretty talkings, nor the life of Christ, the story of his bitter passion; and his incomparable Sermon on the Mount went not into their catechisms. What good can your flocks receive if you discourse well and wisely whether Jephthah sacrificed his daughter, or put her into

[1] Taylor refers here to a large body of Scotch Presbyterians who, trusting to Charles II's declaration in 1662, had taken Irish benefices, but were determined to refuse any co-operation with bishops.

the retirements of a solitary life; nor how David's numbering the people did differ from Joshua's; or whether God took away the life of Moses by an apoplexy, or by the kisses of his mouth?

If scholars be so idly busy in these things in the schools, custom and some other little accidents may help to excuse them; but the time that is spent in your churches and conversation with your people must not be so thrown away: λόγος ἔστω σεμνὸς, that is your rule; "let your speech be grave" and wise, and useful and holy, and intelligible; something to reform their manners, to correct their evil natures, to amend their foolish customs; "to build them up in a most holy faith".

55. THE INSIDIOUS GROWTH OF SIN

So have I seen the little purls of a spring sweat through the bottom of a bank, and intenerate the stubborn pavement, till it hath made it fit for the impression of a child's foot; and it was despised, like the descending purls of a misty morning, till it had opened its way, and made a stream large enough to carry away the ruins of the undermined strand, and to invade the neighbouring gardens; but then the despised drops were grown into an artificial river and an intolerable mischief. . . .

When we see a child strike a servant rudely, or jeer a silly person, or wittingly cheat his play-fellow, or talk words light as the skirt of a summer garment, we laugh and are delighted with the wit and confidence of the boy, and encourage such hopeful beginnings: and in the meantime we consider not, that from these beginnings he shall grow up, till he become a tyrant, an oppressor, a goat, and a traitor. . . . And little boldnesses and looser words, and wranglings for nuts, and lying for trifles, are of the same proportion to the malice of a child, as impudence, and duels, and injurious law-suits, and false witness in judgement, and perjuries, are in men.

56. THE LOVELY EARTH

Is not all the earth our orchard and our granary, our vineyard and our garden of pleasure? And the face of the sea is our traffic, and the bowels of the sea is our vivarium, a place for fish to feed us, and to serve some other collateral appendant needs; and all the face of heaven is a repository for influences and breath, fruitful showers and fair refreshments. . . .

That is a mighty mercy, when the circles of heaven are bowed down to wrap us in a bosom of care and nourishment, and the wisdom of God is daily busied to serve his mercy, as his mercy serves our necessities. Does not God plant remedies there, where the diseases are most popular, and every country is best provided against its own evils? Is not the rhubarb found where the sun most corrupts the liver; and the scabious by the shore of the sea, that God might cure as soon as he wounds? And the inhabitants may see their remedy against the leprosy and the scurvy, before they feel their sickness? And then to this we may add nature's commons and open fields, the shores of rivers and the strand of the sea, the unconfined air, the wilderness that hath no hedge; and that in these every man may hunt, and fowl, and fish, respectively; and that God sends some miracles and extraordinary blessings so for the public good, that he will not endure they should be enclosed and made several.

The poorest artisan of Rome, walking in Cæsar's

gardens, had the same pleasures which they ministered to their lord: and although it may be he was put to gather fruits to eat from another place, yet his other senses were delighted equally with Cæsar's: the birds made him as good music, the flowers gave him as sweet smells; he there sucked as good air, and delighted in the beauty and order of the place, for the same reason and upon the same perception as the prince himself; save only that Cæsar paid for all that pleasure vast sums of money, the blood and treasure of a province, which the poor man had for nothing.

JOHN COSIN (1594–1672)

As a friend of Laud and trusted adherent of Charles I,
Cosin quickly rose to prominence in the Church,
becoming in turn Master of Peterhouse, Cambridge,
Vice-Chancellor of that University, and Dean of
Peterborough.

In 1627 he was asked by the King to draw up a
Collection of Private Devotions for such ladies in Hen-
rietta Maria's household as were Anglicans.

But within a few weeks of his appointment to Peterborough he was impeached by the House of Commons
for superstitious acts and "Popery". In 1642 he sent the
University plate to the King, then at York, and was the
first of many learned and devout Cambridge men to be
deprived of their preferments.

At the King's wish he withdrew in 1643 to Paris to
serve again as chaplain to the Queen's household and
other exiles. In the chapel of Sir Richard Brown, the
British ambassador, he maintained for seventeen years
Anglican services in Paris.

At the Restoration he returned to his Mastership,
and was appointed Bishop of Durham. There he restored cathedral services to great dignity and reverence,
and spent vast sums from his great revenue on restoring
or founding churches, schools, scholarships, and hos-
pitals.

57. A PLEA FOR MORE FREQUENT EUCHARISTS

This[1] to do both morning and evening, as the Church hath enjoined us; and besides this, to give attendance also to all other holy actions that are publicly done and performed in the Church, but especially to the Blessed Sacrament of the Body and Blood of Christ, which, for my part, I think the Church's intention is, as well for the honour of our Saviour as for our own good and benefit, to have celebrated a little oftener than it is.

I say, for the honour of our Saviour—and we are at a holy work when we are honouring him—not only because thereby we submit ourselves to his ordinance, that would have the memory of his precious passion daily preserved till his coming again, but because in this service we honour those things in him, which all the rest of the world besides despised and contemn—I name the humility of his incarnation, the baseness and bitterness of his death, the ignominy of his cross, the multitude of his sufferings—all which we honour and adore—though other miscreants of the world abhor them, and scorn our Saviour for them—in using and frequenting this holy Sacrament.

And it is to be lamented, nay and I trow it is to be amended too, that we honour Christ no oftener this way. Had St Chrysostom lived among us, he would have complained most bitterly against us, not only for defrauding ourselves of many graces and helps that might

[1] I.e., the saying of the Daily Offices.

come to us by the frequent use of it, but also, and that chiefly, for despoiling Christ, as much as in us lies, of his highest and most peculiar honour that he hath reserved to himself, *et cum sit panis quotidianus facitis Eum panem annum*, as he said, "What, come ye once a year to your daily food?", he speaks of the sacrament, which was then called *panis quotidianus*, as well as our own that we feed our bodies with daily; but feed our bodies no oftener with the one than usually we do now our souls with the other, and I trow they will quickly famish. Neither do I know any reason why there should not as good care be taken for the soul, and the due honour of Christ, as there is for the body and the daily respect that we give, and look to be given to ourselves. Sure I am this would keep the day more holy than it useth to be kept without it, for it would be *sancta sanctis*, men would study and give themselves to more holiness upon it; and I would it were so, that the holy Sacrament might always and ever accompany this holy day, and some of you at one time and some at another might assist at that holy, the holiest of all holy services.

58. THE PASSING OF A DEVOUT CHURCHWOMAN

Her conclusion was not different from her premises, nor her death from her life.

Being warned of her danger she showed no dismay, as carrying in her conscience the safe-conduct of innocency; and being not in love with her own desires, she committed herself to the good-will and pleasure of God. Her preparation to her end was by humble contrition, and hearty confession of her sins; which when she had done, she received the benefit of absolution, according to God's ordinance and the religious institution of our Church; a thing that the world looks not after now, as if Confession and Absolution were some strange superstitious things among us, which yet the Church has taken such care to preserve, and especially to be preparatives for death.

When they had given her physic for her body, it presently[1] put her in mind that there was other physic to be taken for her soul; and so she presently sent unto me, who in my priestly function was ready to attend, to have the blessed Sacrament given her, which she received from me with such gladness of her soul, and with such humility and reverence of her body (though she might hardly endure it by reason of her infirmity) that we might easily understand she knew very well what a great Majesty

[1] In Tudor and Stuart times *presently* meant *immediately* (cf. Ps. 46. 1—"God a very present help in trouble").

157

she was then to adore, and what admirable and mysterious benefits she was to receive. Such was her devotion upon the first falling into her last and fatal sickness.

Now the common guise of the world goes another way; as soon as we feel ourselves sick, presently post away all the servants we have, this way and that way for the physicians of our body to come and help us; but for the physicians of our souls, them we never dream on, as if they would do well enough without any physic at all, which yet (God knows) want it ten times more than our bodies do, and are sicker a great deal than they be.

Well, when she was strengthened with this heavenly and spiritual repast, she set herself to combat with death. And whereas others use to be so much afraid to meddle with it, she was not one whit dismayed; but showing her willingness to be dissolved and to be with Christ, often in mine own hearing desired that death would come to her to bring her out of these miseries to the joys of Heaven. Nor was she so disposed as many are, call for death to make us believe that they are willing to die, and then wish it gone again when it comes; like as Laertius tells us the story of Antisthenes, a philosopher, that led his life well, and was loth to part with it, if he knew how to have kept it, though he seemed to others to be desirous to be rid of it. The man, being tied to his bed by a grievous disease, was visited by Diogenes, that knowing the nature of him very well, had taken a sword with him under his gown. As soon as ever he comes in, Antisthenes looks upon him, and cries out for pity, "O God," says he, "who will deliver me from hence?" "Marry, that will I," says Diogenes presently, and so shews him the sword in his hand, "this shall do it." "O God," says Antisthenes, "no, no, I mean from my pains, and not from my life"; he was loth to part with that, whatsoever he said. So Esop tells us of an old man that being laden with a great burden and fallen into a ditch and lying there a long time without hope, at last calls aloud for Death. Well, Death comes to him, and bids him go along with him; "O no," says he, "I call thee to help me up with my burden, that I may return"; he was loth to stand to his word too.

But for her now, her willingness that she had professed at first, she continued to her last day; and when death came, it was welcome to her; she made no reluctation at all. And though she had sore pangs upon her by reason of her long sickness, yet God gave her such patience to endure it as it was almost a marvel to us that saw it. During the time of her sickness, which was a long while together, she offered up with us the continual sacrifice of prayer to God, both morning and evening and at noonday, besides her continual ejaculations. She made open profession of her faith, and she died a true member of the Church, and the child of God. She enjoyed her judgement as long as she breathed, and when her tongue could speak no longer, her thoughts offered up her last devotions; and so, while the penitential Psalms were read over her, she eftsoons went to God: and as one rather fallen asleep than dying, she most happily took her leave of all mortal miseries.

ISAAC BARROW (1630–77)

After an unsuccessful beginning at Charterhouse (where he was found too pugnacious) the boy Barrow developed at Felsted as a phenomenon of industry and brilliant genius in mathematics and science. Then, studying at Trinity College, Cambridge, he was likely to have been made Professor of Greek to the University, had not his strong Royalist opinions driven him into four years' exile on the Continent.

At the Restoration he obtained the Greek professorship, and a little later he became Professor of Geometry, and in turn the first Lucasian Professor of Mathematics. His mathematical books were written in Latin. All learning seemed to come alike to him; and when in 1672 Charles II offered him the Mastership of Trinity College, he said it was to "the best scholar in England". Isaac Newton was one of Barrow's pupils.

Barrow's sermons were written in the calm and reasoned style which gradually ousted the impassioned prose of the earlier Caroline preachers and won him the name of "the perfect preacher". A reader who studies his second quotation here will mark his pure English, his convincing arguments, his sound logic. But men's minds are not easily persuaded by pure logic. "Barrow," says W. Fraser Mitchell, "though his preaching throughout is characterized by strong personal devotion to the Saviour, could voice his reflections on God as follows: 'ὁ Θεὸς γεωμετρεῖ! *Tu autem Domine, quantus es Geometra!*'"

His somewhat icy style ignored the human heart, and led to the perfectly smooth and unemotional prose of Tillotson, whose sermons, pleasing in themselves, dealt with ethics rather than with the Gospel. This perfecting of unimpassioned pulpit prose led in turn to the decay of English preaching, broken at last only by the trumpet-call of Whitefield and the Wesleys.

59. OPPOSITION OF THE HUMAN WILL TO GOD

What faculty of our soul or member of our body is not obsequious to our will? Even half the resolution with which we pursue vanity and sin would serve to engage us in the ways of wisdom and virtue.

Wherefore in overcoming our will the stress lieth; this is that impregnable fortress, which everlastingly doth hold out against all the batteries of reason and of grace; which no force of persuasion, no allurement of favour, no discouragement of terror can reduce: this puny, this impotent thing it is, which grappleth with omnipotency and often in a manner baffleth it. And no wonder; for that God doth not intend to overpower our will, or to make any violent impression on it, but only to "draw it" (as it is in the Prophet) "with the cords of a man", or by rational inducements to win its consent and compliance; our service is not so considerable to him, that he should extort it from us; nor doth he value our happiness at so low a rate as to obtrude it on us. His victory indeed were no true victory over us, if he should gain it by main force, or without the concurrence of our will; our works not being our works, if they do not issue from our will; and our will not being our will, if it be not free; to compel it were to destroy it, together with all the worth of our virtue and obedience: wherefore the Almighty doth suffer himself to be withstood, and beareth repulses from us; nor commonly doth he master our will otherwise than by its own spontaneous conversion and submission to him. If ever we be conquered, as we shall share in the benefit, and wear a crown; so we must join in the combat, and partake of the victory, by subduing ourselves: *we must take the yoke upon us*; for God is only served by volunteers; he summoneth us by his Word, he attracteth us by his Grace, but we must *freely come unto him*.

Our will indeed of all things is most our own; the only gift, the most proper sacrifice we have to offer; which therefore God doth chiefly desire, doth most highly prize, doth most kindly accept from us. Seeing then our duty moveth chiefly on this hinge, the free submission and resignation of our will to the will of God; it is this practice, which our Lord (who came to guide us in the way to happiness, not only as a teacher by his word and excellent doctrine, but as a leader, by his actions and perfect example) did especially set before us; as in the constant tenor of his life, so particularly in that great exigency which occasioned these words (*Nevertheless let not my will, but thine be done*), wherein, renouncing and deprecating his own will, he did express an entire submission to God's will, a hearty complacence therein, and a serious desire that it might take place.

60. A PEACEFUL TONGUE ADDS
WEIGHT TO ARGUMENT

In defence of truth and maintenance of a good cause, we
may observe that commonly the fairest language is most
proper and advantageous, and that reproachful or foul
terms are most improper and prejudicial. A calm and
meek way of discoursing doth much advantage a good
cause, as arguing the patron thereof to have confidence
in the cause itself, and to rely upon his strength; that he is
in a temper fit to apprehend it himself, and to maintain
it; that he propoundeth it as a friend, wishing the hearer
for his own good to follow it, leaving him the liberty
to judge and choose for himself. But rude speech and
contemptuous reflections on persons, as they do signify
nothing to the question, so they commonly bring much
disadvantage and damage to the cause, creating mighty
prejudices against it. They argue much impotency in the
advocate, and consequently little strength in what he
maintains; that he is little able to judge well, and altogether unapt to teach others. They intimate a diffidence
in himself concerning his cause, and that, despairing to
maintain it by reason, he seeks to uphold it by passion;
that, not being able to convince by fair means, he would
bear down by noise and clamour; that, not skilling to get
his suit quietly, he would extort it by force, obtruding
his conceits violently as an enemy, or imposing them
arbitrarily as a tyrant. Thus doth he really disparage and
slur his cause, however good and defensible in itself.

A modest and friendly style doth suit truth; it, like its author, doth usually reside (not in the rumbling *wind*, nor in the shaking *earthquake*, nor in the raging *fire*, but, in the *small still voice*; sounding in this, it is most audible, most penetrant, and most effectual: thus propounded, it is willingly hearkened unto; for men have no aversation from hearing those who seem to love them and wish them well. It is easily conceived; no prejudice or passion clouding the apprehensive faculties; it is readily embraced; no animosity withstanding or obstructing it. It is *the sweetness of the lips*, which (as the Wise Man telleth us) *increaseth learning*; disposing a man to hear lessons of good doctrine, rendering him capable to understand them, insinuating and impressing them upon the mind. The affections being thereby unlocked, the passage becomes open to the Reason. . . .

Every man (saith the wise man) shall *kiss his lips that giveth a right answer*: but no man surely will be ready to kiss those lips which are embittered with reproach, or defiled with dirty language.

It is said of Pericles, that *with thundering and lightning he put Greece into confusion*: such discourse may serve to confound things, it seldom tendeth to compose them. If Reason will not pierce, Rage will scarce avail to drive it in. Satirical virulency may vex men sorely, but it hardly ever soundly converts them. *Few become wiser or better by ill words*. Children may be frighted into compliance by loud and severe increpations; but men are to be allured by rational persuasion backed with courteous usage: they may be sweetly drawn, they cannot be violently driven to change their judgement and practice. Whence that advice of the Apostle, *With meekness instruct those that oppose themselves*, doth no less savour of wisdom than of goodness.

BIBLIOGRAPHY

Andrewes, Lancelot, *XCVI Sermons*. Parker, 1841.

Barrow, Isaac, *Theological Works*. 8 vols. Clarendon Press, 1830.

Cosin, John, *Works*. 2 vols. of *Sermons* (Anglo-Catholic Library). Parker, 1849.

Donne, John, *Works*. 6 vols., ed. H. Alford. Parker, 1839.

Frank, Mark, *A Year's Sermons*. 2 vols. (Anglo-Catholic Library). Parker, 1849.

Hammond, Henry, *Sermons*. 2 vols. (Anglo-Catholic Library). Parker, 1849.

Taylor, Jeremy, *Whole Works*. 15 vols., ed. R. Heber. Parker, 1822.

Bunyan, John, *Grace Abounding* (autobiography). 1666, many editions since.

Walton, Izaak, *Lives* of Donne, Wotton, Hooker, Herbert, and Sanderson. 1640–78, many editions since.

Biographical Dictionary of English Literature. Dent (Everyman's Library), 1910, several editions since.

Baxter, Richard, *Autobiography*, ed. Lloyd Thomas. Dent (Everyman's Library), 1931.

Bosher, R. S., *The Making of the Restoration Settlement: The Influence of the Laudians, 1649–62*. Dacre Press, 1951.

Buchan, John, *Oliver Cromwell*. Hodder, 1934.

BIBLIOGRAPHY

Carr, J. A., *Life and Times of Archdeacon Ussher*. Wells Gardner, 1895.

Donne's Sermons: Selected Passages, ed. Logan Pearsall Smith. Clarendon Press, 1920.

Gosse, Edmund, *Jeremy Taylor*. Macmillan, 1904.

Henson, Hensley, *Puritanism in England*. Hodder, 1912.

Herbert, George, *The Temple* and *A Priest to the Temple*. Dent (Everyman's Library), 1908.

Hooker, Richard, *Laws of Ecclesiastical Polity*, Vol. V. Dent (Everyman's Library), 1907.

Hutton, W. H., "Caroline Divines" (*Cambridge History of English Literature*, Vol. VI, ch. 7). 1911.

—, *The English Church 1625–1714* (Vol. VI of Stephens' and Hunt's *History of the English Church*). Macmillan, 1903.

—, *William Laud*. Methuen, 1895.

Jessopp, Augustus, *John Donne*. Methuen, 1897.

Maycock, A. L., *Nicholas Ferrar of Little Gidding*. S.P.C.K., 1938.

Mitchell, W. F., *English Pulpit Oratory from Andrewes to Tillotson*. S.P.C.K., 1932.

Morley, Henry, *Illustrations of English Religion* (Vol. II of Cassell's Library of English Literature). 1890.

Mozley, J. B., "Laud" (*Essays Historical and Theological*, Vol. I). Rivington's, 1884.

Osmond, P. H., *Issac Barrow*. S.P.C.K., 1944.

Ottley, R. L., *Lancelot Andrewes*. Methuen, 1894.

Palgrave, M. E., *Mary Rich, Countess of Warwick*. Dent, 1901.

BIBLIOGRAPHY

Richardson, C. F., *English Preachers and Preaching: A Secular Study*. S.P.C.K., 1928.

Selected English Sermons: 16th to 19th Centuries, with an Introduction by H. Hensley Henson. World's Classics, 1939.

Simpkinson, C. H., *Life and Times of William Laud*. John Murray, 1894.

Stephen, James, "Richard Baxter" (*Essays in Ecclesiastical Biography*, Vol. II). Longmans, 1907.

Stranks, C. J., *Life and Writings of Jeremy Taylor*. S.P.C.K., 1952.

SOURCES

(For details of the works printed in italics see Bibliography)

LANCELOT ANDREWES
XCVI Sermons, 1841

1:	Sermon 6 of the Nativity
2:	Sermon 5 of the Nativity
3:	Sermon 14 of the Resurrection
4:	Sermon 5 of Repentance and Fasting
5:	Sermon 1 of the Passion
6:	Sermon 1 of Repentance and Fasting

JOHN DONNE
Works of John Donne, 1839

7:	Volume III	Sermon 60
8:	Volume III	Sermon 64
9:	Volume III	Sermon 66
10:	Volume III	Sermon 64
11:	Volume III	Sermon 71
12(a):	Volume III	Sermon 80
(b):	Volume I	Sermon 9
13:	Volume IV	Sermon 109
14:	Volume III	Sermon 76
15:	Volume III	Sermon 66
16:	Volume VI	Sermon 158
17:	Volume III	Sermon 76
18:	Volume III	Sermon 76

SOURCES

JOHN DONNE—*continued*.

19:	Volume III	Sermon 75
20:	Volume III	Sermon 66
21:	Volume IV	Sermon 81
22:	Volume IV	Sermon 83
23:	Volume III	Sermon 66
24:	Volume IV	Sermon 92
25:	Volume II	Sermon 31
26:	Volume II	Sermon 34
27:	Volume IV	Sermon 83
28:	Volume III	Sermon 76

JOHN HALES

29:	*Selected English Sermons*, 1939
30:	Ibid.
31:	*Illustrations of English Religion*, 1890

HENRY HAMMOND
Sermons, 1849

32:	Volume I	Sermon 28

MARK FRANK
A Year's Sermons, 1849

33:	Volume II	Sermon 30
34:	Volume II	Sermon 30
35:	Volume II	Sermon 30
36:	Volume I	Sermon 6
37:	Volume I	Sermon 1

MARK FRANK—*continued.*

38:	Volume I	Sermon 25
39:	Volume II	Sermon 33
40:	Volume II	Sermon 38
41:	Volume II	Sermon 39
42:	Volume I	Sermon 4
43:	Volume II	Sermon 48
44:	Volume I	Sermon 2

JEREMY TAYLOR

Whole Works, 1822

45:	Volume V (Twenty-five Sermons)	Sermon 18
46:	Volume V (Twenty-five Sermons)	Sermon 17
47:	Volume V (Twenty-five Sermons)	Sermon 2
48:	Volume V (Twenty-five Sermons)	Sermon 5
49:	Volume V (Thirteen Sermons)	Sermon 9
50:	Volume V (Twenty-five Sermons)	Sermon 6
51:	Volume V (Twenty-five Sermons)	Sermon 6
52:	Volume VI	Sermon 25
53:	Volume V (Thirteen Sermons)	Sermon 12
54:	Volume VI (Ten Sermons)	Sermon 10
55:	Volume VI	Sermon 16
56:	Volume VI	Sermons 26 and 18

JOHN COSIN

Sermons, 1849

57:	Volume I	Sermon 13
58:	Volume I	Sermon 2 (Funeral Sermon, Mrs Holmes)

SOURCES

ISAAC BARROW

Theological Works, 1830